JESSE JAMES:

THE MAKING OF A LEGEND

by

Larry C. Bradley

Larren 〔LP〕 *Publishers* ®

Nevada, Missouri 1980

1

Copyright © 1980 by Larren Publishers

Library of Congress Catalog Card Number 80-81622

ISBN: 0-9604370-0-2

Printed in the United States of America by
Litho Printers, Cassville, Mo.

First Edition

Dedicated with admiration and affection

to my wife, Karen

ACKNOWLEDGMENTS

In addition to the many persons cited below, there are people who deserve special credit for having helped me in the actual preparation of this book. Without this devotion, it would not have been possible to finish it on time. The first of these is my wife, Karen, who proofread the manuscript, and helped ameliorate the stress around me; and Robert B. McCarthy, who assisted in the selection of the photo illustrations and provided moral support.

I am also indebted to Twentieth Century-Fox Film Corporation.

Those who have been of assistance to me include: Joseph C. Behm, Clark Bradley, Flossie Bradley, Dabbs Greer, Gene M. Gressley, Nunnally Johnson, Henry King, William Morgan, Frank Powlny, Cheri Taylor, Don Walker, and Velma Williams. To them, and others who requested anonymity, my deepest thanks.

Among the institutions that have been of assistance to me are the American Heritage Center at University of Wyoming, Laramie; McDonald County Missouri Library, Pineville; Missouri State Library, Jefferson City; Nevada Missouri Public Library; Springfield-Greene County Missouri Library; and State Historical Society of Missouri, Columbia.

PROLOGUE

During the 1930's, for people who could spare a dime or a quarter, America was a kingdom of motion picture palaces. It was a time when the novelty of sound had worn off, audiences were more selective as their incomes sank, and they demanded from the Hollywood studios that movies be made with a story, a message, and realism so they could escape for a brief respite the desperation and unrest of the Depression. But it was also a time for social commentary. There was *Let Us Live* that explored a real story of law and order gone awry in the false arrest and near execution of two taxi drivers. And there was *Angels With Dirty Faces, Angels Wash Their Faces,* and *They Made Me A Criminal*, which had a way of looking at the causes for criminal behavior through the eyes of the identifiable, real, poor people who stood the farthest from Wall Street.

Audiences were oriented to the notion of society being the ultimate villain because it had tremendous appeal to the ordinary person. That made it easy for Darryl F. Zanuck to bring *Jesse James* to the screen with Tyrone Power portraying Jesse and Henry Fonda cast as Frank James.

Yet, it was this single event that changed Pineville, a quiet southwestern Missouri town of no more than five hundred, into a star struck city of fifty thousand people. This was still Depression country in 1938 and the natives of the area lived a hand-to-mouth existence. Cash was scarce, jobs were nonexistent, and no one had ever dreamed of welfare and social security, which would arrive a few years later. All of a sudden, there were jobs and cash like no one had ever seen before and the prevailing sentiment, "We never had nuthin', so we never knowed what we wuz missin' " was thrown aside.

Too soon, it was over. The cast and crew packed up and went back to Hollywood and the natives went back to the hills, raising meager crops and cattle on their rocky land. The glittering world of make believe came to an end. And the flow of cash ceased.

For years, Pineville folks kept asking "When are those Hollywood people goin' to make another movie out here?" They did, but

7

only once, to film a few background scenes for *Belle Starr*.

Today, the town has an annual Jesse James Day celebration. Hundreds of people turn out each July to watch the movie and see their grandfathers and grandmothers, or uncles and aunts, who worked as extras in the film, alive again in technicolor.

And for a few days the town and people reminisce the time when Twentieth Century-Fox came and made a picture.

Nevada, Missouri   Larry C. Bradley
May, 1980

I

JESSE JAMES, THE MAN

Like all great men, Frank and Jesse were both born "wi' a wudden ladle in their mouths...no silver spoon..." and given by God, "the virtue, temper, understanding, taste, that lifted them into life, and let them fall just in the niche they were ordain'd to fill."

Jesse James was a fortunate man; that is, if he wanted to be regarded as a legend and thus immortalized in movies. No other American criminal has so deeply etched his imprint upon our culture as Jesse James, a man sparsely documented yet with a definite personality. Jesse has long ceased to be a private person and will never pass into obscurity simply because heroes, as Gerald White Johnson once said, "are created by popular demand, sometimes out of the scantiest materials...such as the apple that William Tell never shot, the ride that Paul Revere never finished, the flag that Barbara Frietchie never waved." Heroes—and villains—live forever in stories which were shaped and polished by the hazards of oral transmission and later recorded by anthologists emphasizing their importance in literature.

No doubt the ancestors of these stories were once asked to explain the phenomena that surrounded and puzzled the backwoods humorists and his audience, or to authenticate customs and beliefs. This latter fact combined with the ancestry of its early inhabitants has provided an opportunity for Missouri to give its share of legends and folk stories to the world. It is famously known as the "Mother of the West" because it was from Missouri that the pioneers first ventured out on the Santa Fe and Oregon Trails. The geographical boundaries are somewhat fuzzy, but the rugged surface features of this area aided in keeping alive many legends and tales. But there is only one outlaw—Jesse James.

The facts about the life of this strange, shadowy individual are few, and if only the facts that can be accepted as approximate truth are those attested to by his defamers and panegyrists, even less is known concerning his personality, regarding in a vital sense, his character. It did not matter that Jesse was a mere mortal; the legend was stronger than his mortality. Carl Sandburg recognized it, saying, "There is only one American bandit (Jesse James) who is classical, who is to the country what Robin Hood and Dick Turpin are to England, whose exploits are so close to the mythical and apocryphal."

Theodore Roosevelt wrote, "There is something very curious in the reproduction here in this new continent of essentially the condition

11

of ballad growth which was obtained in medieval England; including, by the way, sympathy for the outlaw, Jesse James, taking the place of Robin Hood."

Was Jesse a saint or a devil, a hero or a villain, a patriot or a rascal, a chivalrous knight or a dragon in human form—or was he an insoluble compound of such opposites? Was he a brave soul fighting against inauspicious destiny, or was he a low scoundrelly chap, courageous to be sure, but repulsive and brutal, a murderer or a cutthroat, who killed just for the fun of killing? Jesse James never lived at all; he was a pure creation of the mind. He was born, he lived, and he died, in the complex of far-reaching imagination of his race. He was an ordinary fellow in his mundane life, probably, like most of us, but it was his fortune to be transformed beyond recognition into the demon-god of his time, and to be endowed with fantastic and chimerical qualities—to be the "Great American Myth" and a legend while he still lived in the flesh.

Jesse is reputed to have presented $1,500 to an impoverished widow who was about to be turned out of her rickety cabin—and to have repossessed himself of the amount by robbing the man who held the mortgage. But this is hearsay, and so is the story that Jesse enticed a posse to follow him. Either instance could, of course, be true; but the story of the James brothers is so entwined in fact and fiction that it is impossible to unravel them.

Accompanied by three men, Jesse once rode up to the ticket office of the Kansas City Fair. He dismounted and approached it saying, "What if I was to say I was Jesse James and told you to hand out that tin box of money, what would you say?"

"I'd say I'd see you in hell first," was the contemptuous reply.

"Well, that's just who I am," and he helped himself to $10,000.

A Kansas City newspaper hailed the robbery as "so diabolically daring and so utterly in contempt of fear that we are bound to admire it and revere its perpetrators." Two days later, the paper compared the James brothers to the Knights of King Arthur's Round Table:

It was as though three bandits had come to us from storied Odenwald, with the halo of medieval chivalry upon their garments, and shown us how the things were done that poets sing of. Nowhere else in the United States or in the civilized world, probably, could this thing have been done.

On another occasion, a politician was making a long-winded speech on the proposed railroad, new school building, and the evils of black Republicanism to a large audience at Corydon, Iowa. At some point, a mysterious bearded stranger interrupted by crying, "A point, sir." Thinking the man wished to ask a question, the speaker replied, "You may interrupt, if it's important."

"Well, sir," drawled the stranger, "I reckon it's important enough. The fact is some fellows have been over to the bank and tied up the cashier. All of the drawers are cleaned out. You folks best get down there and untie him. I've got to be getting along."

No one believed him until he and his gang had ridden off, and then it was too late, as they discovered. "My God, it was the James gang! They just robbed the bank!"

The naive stories, such as "The James Boys Brides," "The Man on the Black Horse," "Jesse, the Outlaw," "The James Boys in a Fix," and "Frank Reade, the Inventor, Chasing the James Boys with His Steam Train," are endless and probably a large percentage of Jesse's folklore legends were churned out in pamphlet-sized novellas called dime novels. These pulp magazines were read by America's male population, before the turn of the century, in brothels, saloons, and barbershops, who believed that Jesse and his men were simple farmers driven to the gun by unscrupulous, vindictive, and often sadistic lawmen.

Jesse's moods could be precarious and quite charming, with chivalrous manners, although he spoke rarely, preferring deeds to words, and then suddenly he was transformed into an implacable murderer. He used liquor, tobacco, and bad language sparingly, loved his mother devotedly, and demonstrated the same elegant style when robbing trains and banks simultaneously while protecting forlorn women and children. Jesse enjoyed the sympathy not only of his acquaintances, but also of a large portion of the people throughout the state of Missouri. The dramatic unities are at times necessarily disregarded, and the protagonist does not stand out as sharply as would be desirable; but the vast panorama of action, and the obscuring shadows that have fallen quickly upon various points of the story, preclude a clear-cut and well-rounded performance. And it is in this latter guise, naturally enough, that Hollywood chose to depict the outlaw in the motion picture *Jesse James*, in 1938.

Like all great men, Frank and Jesse were both born "wi' a wudden ladle in their mouths...no silver spoon..." and given by God, "the virtue, temper, understanding, taste, that lifted them into life, and let them fall just in the niche they were ordain'd to fill."

Frank, christened Alexander Franklin on the day of his birth, 10 January 1843, and Jesse Woodson James, 5 September 1847, were the sons of Robert and Zerelda Cole James, who had migrated from Kentucky to the Missouri frontier in 1842. The courtship of this couple began when Robert was a theological student at Georgetown College and Zerelda was attending a Roman Catholic convent in Lexington where her guardian had placed her. They were married on 28 December 1841.

After his graduation, Robert and Zerelda traveled to Clay County, Missouri, to visit her mother, who was living there with her second husband. Here they decided to homestead and began to carve from the wilderness a modest 275 acre farm near the small and struggling community of Kearney. Robert took over the pastorate of New Hope Baptist Church and alternated between farming and a circuit-riding ministry, establishing several small churches which still exist. In his ministerial travels, he realized the need for a fundamental Christian school, and was instrumental in founding William Jewell College, at nearby Liberty. He served on the college's first board of trustees, although its officials have been reluctant to publicize the fact.

When he was not tending the souls of his parishioners, Robert tried to make a living out of farming, but not making much money, the family went hungry. Although Zerelda was devoutly religious in her own way, she did not share her husband's enthusiasm for the ministry. Her objections to his absence from home so annoyed Robert that in a final bid to improve their fortunes he joined, on 2 April 1850, a caravan of gold seekers and started the long journey to California, leaving behind his hard-pressed family. Zerelda had a premonition that she would never see him again, and she never did. Less than three weeks after his arrival, he contracted pneumonia and died.

Robert's death left Zerelda with the responsibility of supporting her children, and struggling to work the land. Times were rough and she allowed her next-door neighbor, Benjamin Simms, to propose to her. The marriage did not succeed. Simms wanted her property transferred to him, but after quarrelling incessantly they separated.

There are two versions for the brevity of this union. One has Zerelda insisting that Simms treated his stepsons, Frank and Jesse, cruelly; the other has the farmer declaring he "could not stand" her rambunctious brats. In those days divorce was not entered into lightly, but Zerelda was saved the trouble of obtaining one when Simms obligingly fell off a horse and died of his injuries.

For her third excursion into matrimony, she married Dr. Reuben Samuel, a mild-mannered general practitioner and farmer, in September 1855. The docile doctor and his stormy self-assertive wife succeeded from the start, basically because he was a close-lipped type, who kept to this work, and was a good father to her children. In due course she increased her tally of children to four.

Whatever clashes of personality may have existed in the James-Samuel household it is too absurd to suggest that Frank and Jesse's criminal tendencies had been transmitted to them by their mother. One anonymous author declared, in *The Wild Bandits of the Border,* that "of the milk of human kindness they had none, for they had drunk in from their earliest days only bitterness and malice and hatred with the most remorseless cruelty." There is no evidence to depict them any differently than normal boys of their time and circumstance.

Frank was the family favorite, called "Mr. Frank," by his mother; neighbors afterwards recalled him as studious, slow and calculating of speech, but well read, frequently quoting from the Bible or Shakespeare. Although he was corpulently built, colorless, and slightly crouched, he could ride further, faster, and subsist on less food portions than any other gang member. He claimed not to enjoy being an outlaw or relish killing for killing's sake. Looking back on his life, Frank once recalled, "I have literally lived in the saddle. I have never known a day of perfect peace. It was one long, anxious, inexorable, eternal vigil." If, as seems likely, Jesse was a natural, stubborn and rebellious leader with a quick, ingratiating charm, Frank was not. Several authorities have credited him as being the brains and leader of the gang, but the lack of documentation cannot verify this unequivocally. Nevertheless, when Jesse beckoned, Frank would come obediently regardless where he was at the time.

Meanwhile, hostilities intensified between braggart Southerners and militant abolitionists in the Northeast over the course of slavery with the counties above the Missouri-Kansas border as an exacerbating dress rehearsal for war. The continuance of slavery in Western territories had long been a matter of contention in the dispute between the two sections. A balance had been sustained in the Senate by systematically admitting free and slave states, and neither section wanted the equality upset in the other's favor. The immense region acquired by the United States in the Louisiana Purchase had precipitated a lengthly power struggle that was finally resolved in 1820 by the Missouri Compromise. This "dauntless spirit of resolution" permitted Missouri to enter the Union as a slave state, but did not allow slavery in the remainder of the territory north of latitude 36° 30', the line that formed the southern boundary of Missouri. To preserve sectional balance, the act had also sanctioned the admittance of Maine as a free state. It did little to repel the wave of fanaticism that threatened to break up the Union.

Frank and Jesse were too young to enlist; nevertheless, that bitter fraticidal strife was directly responsible for determining their future. Those fiery abolitionists, who prevailed with the sentiment, "we want no slaves, and no niggers," flocked to Kansas in the early 1850's, formed a marauding band, euphoniously called Jayhawkers and Red Legs, which harassed the proslaveryites for various reasons—self-protection, patriotism, proselytism, and plunder. These atrocities led to an organization of guerrillas under William Clarke Quantrill, a former schoolteacher from Maryland, who inflamed his followers with the Biblical cry "an eye for an eye and a tooth for a tooth."

Perhaps Jesse would have followed in his father's footsteps and made his mark in the pulpit had the Civil War not occurred. But the bitter confrontation between the slavery factions bent the James brothers toward the Southern cause. Numerous stories of Jayhawker atrocities circulated and Quantrill made their blood boil, enticing them with the incessant need to requite. The first clash between Union troops and Rebel guerrillas in Missouri occurred on 30 April 1861 with the seizure of the Federal Arsenal at Liberty. On 4 May, a militia of Home Guards was organized at Kearney. Frank, then eighteen, enlisted.

Several months later, Frank received a furlough and went home. He was reported to have brandished a pistol somewhat pretentiously in Liberty to accentuate his political leanings for the Southern cause.

16

Local indignation resulted in his being incarcerated in jail. The Unionists were lenient in those early months of the war, and offered him amnesty provided he never again bear arms against the United States.

Frank James gained his parole, went back home, fretted about his inactivity, and decided to go back to war, after the provisional government issued an order "that every man of military age was to enroll in the state militia, subject to call for service by the commanding officer of the Department of Missouri." This time he saw the opportunity for adventure and decided to join Quantrill's guerrillas, one of the bloodiest forces along the border states.

Frank was with Quantrill at Lawrence, Kansas, but despite legend, there is no evidence that Jesse had joined the guerrilla band. It seems that Jesse, just turned seventeen, was ordered home.

The Quantrill raid on Lawrence was devastating. Within four hours, the town was in ashes and 142 men lay dead. Only women and children had been spared. Frank's behavior on this occasion was described as "ferocious and merciless as a hyena." Between the looting and the property destroyed by fire, the estimated loss was placed at two million dollars.

Retaliation occurred a short time later when Unionists in their pursuit of vengeance, marched to the Samuel's farm attempting to locate Frank James. They had kept it under surveillance and knew that it was a well-known meeting place for Quantrill's men, and that Jesse and Zerelda had carried messages and served as lookouts for the guerrillas. Dr. Samuel refused to divulge his whereabouts and was abruptly informed of their intention to hang him "for disloyal remarks and friendship with Quantrill." They seized, bound him, tied a rope around his neck, threw the end over a tree, and yanked him off the ground three times, which rendered him unconscious. When Jesse went to his aid, he was whipped with ropes and taken off to prison in Liberty. Still failing to get information, Jesse was released.

Returning home, Jesse became more outspoken and daring in expression and act, which resulted in a subsequent visit, several weeks later, by the Unionists. Fortunately both Jesse and Dr. Samuel were away, but Zerelda and his sister were taken into custody. Their theory was that, once he heard about it, Frank James would attempt a rescue. But he never did. After two months in prison and no definite charges against them, the women were released. This ill-treatment of his family so enraged Jesse that it hardened his determination to find Frank and join Quantrill's guerrillas.

Jesse found Frank, and it was his intervention that persuaded Quantrill to let him join the contingent led by "Bloody Bill" Anderson. It was not an act of loyalty to a cause, because he was motivated by a personal vengeance to kill as many Unionists as he could.

On one occasion, Jesse was disguised as a girl and sent by Anderson to a certain brothel frequented by Union troops. He managed to convince the Madam that he (she) wanted to escape the tedium of home and have a little innocent fun. Madam laughed and was quite pleased. The shameful festival was at its height with nude women, heavy drinking, loud and lewd songs. Suddenly, this disgraceful corybantic revel was disturbed by a blood-curdling cry and twelve soldiers lay dead.

The Civil War ended with an amnesty issued for guerrillas. Jesse, leading a band of six raiders, including Frank James and Cole Younger, met in a council of war and decided to relinquish their arms. They rode into Lexington, Missouri, under a white flag to fix terms of dispensation, and were marching out when a company of eight federal troops intercepted them and opened fire, probably having mistaken the flag of truce for the much-disputed rebel banner. Jesse was wounded when a bullet pierced his right lung, but he managed to crawl away to safety.

For two days Jesse lay delirious on a creek bank, soothing his wounds, until a farmer found him and gave him medical attention. The next day he helped Jesse to travel to Rulo, Nebraska, where Dr. Samuel and his family had settled after they were forced by Unionists to abandon their farm. For some time he believed he was going to die and insistently begged his mother to take him back to Missouri. Zerelda reluctantly acquiesced and transported her son to Harlem, Missouri, by way of the Missouri river. He was taken off the river boat on a stretcher and removed to a lodginghouse owned by his uncle, John Mimms. Jesse probably would have died, had it not been for the devoted nursing of his sister, Susan, and a cousin, Zee.

While the war animosities and political strife diminished, Frank and Jesse were endeavoring to mend their lives. Comparatively little is known, except that the James boys lived at their mother's home marking time. What was their future to be? No military habitation existed and the prospect of an ordinary profession was inconceivable. In all probability, neither could comprehend the terrible strain of inaction or the adjustment to the calm of postwar life. Slowly, their warped and hardened minds rationalized the need to avenge mistreatment by others. They turned to outlawry, with no pretense to honesty, as did hundreds who were victims of circumstance.

The James boys picked the Clay County Savings Bank of Liberty for their first target as professional bank robbers. The date was 13 February 1866. That afternoon a dozen riders drifted into town and converged nonchalantly on the square. All of them were muffled in long, blue soldiers' overcoats, and some wore six-shooters buckled outside their coats. The first three riders dismounted, taking up strategic positions from which they could observe the surrounding streets. The rest rode up in front of the bank and two dismounted and sauntered into the small bank.

Inside, a clerk and cashier were toiling over the account books. The cashier saw the two strangers step beside the stove as if to warm themselves. The clerk continued to work, unaware of their presence. After a moment one of the men walked toward them and said, "I'd like to change a ten dollar bill."

"Well gentlemen...," replied the clerk.

But before he could finish the stranger had pulled out his gun and, almost as a second thought, enlarged his demand. "I'd like all the money in the bank and quickly," he said.

Once he had collected the gold, silver, greenbacks and bonds from the cashier, the gang rode out of town wheeling about like cavalry preparing for a charge, brandishing their pistols and intimidating the town with their shooting. The object was to deter any pursuit. Unfortunately, one of the bullets killed a youth who was scurrying to safety. A few days later, the youth's parents received a note signed by Frank and Jesse James, in which they expressed regret for the accident.

The reckless slaying was tragic enough, but the unbelievable fact was the realization that the bank had been robbed in broad daylight. No one had ever done anything like it before to an American bank, except for a raid on a bank in Vermont by Confederate guerrillas during the Civil War. Jesse James had conceived the idea, and set a pattern for others to follow.

By the time a posse could be formed, a blinding snowstorm that had swept over the countryside had obliterated the gangs' tracks and made them impossible to follow. The storm-battered posse returned to Liberty and told townspeople, "Not a sign of them. We searched all day."

Jesse James did not keep a log of his bank, railroad, and stagecoach robberies; and Frank wrote no memoirs. Consequently, Jesse and Frank were accused of many crimes, but law-enforcement officials lacked evidence to support their allegations. Their alibis were always the same. They could not have done it as they were home tending to chores. Loose-tongued neighbors who identified them during these raids suddenly became tight-lipped when the lawmen started asking questions. Nowhere in Western Missouri was it safe for a person who threatened them, because they had methods of terrorizing witnesses and suppressing evidence by threats. This silent conspiracy became the way of life around Liberty, continuing until Jesse's death.

As Frank and Jesse's felonious goings-on intensified, the authorities began to take them seriously. Among the law-enforcement agencies pitted against them was the Pinkerton Detective Agency who soon discovered that they were dealing with a "craftier, sterner breed of men than the country bumpkins of Indiana."

The Pinkerton Agency had lost three operatives in their pursuit of the James brothers and it was in January 1875 that this outfit committed one of the biggest blunders of its long career. For a considerable time, a Pinkerton agent had been keeping a close eye on the Samuel home, and learned that Frank and Jesse were planning to spend a couple of weeks with their mother. When he passed the news on to his superiors, they wasted no time getting into action to flush the brothers from their cover.

Arrangements were made with the superintendent of the Hannibal and St. Joseph Railroad to ready a special train for the posse. The train left Union Station, Kansas City, with only the conductor knowing its destination. His orders were to stop at the crossroad two miles south of Kearney, let the posse disembark, and then continue on to Lathrop. By a coincidence, he was to meet and be killed by Jesse James in another train robbery several years later.

Without incident, the posse made their way to the Samuel farm. The weather was perfectly clear; it was a bright, moonlit, and bitterly cold night, the silence broken only by the horses champing on their bits. On checking the stables they found two horses inside showing signs of just having been ridden. The house was in darkness, except for the faint glow from a fireplace, indicating the occupants were asleep.

Suddenly, one of the Pinkerton agents called out to those inside to open up and be questioned, but they refused to comply. Shortly afterwards two men sneaked up to the living room window. Their task was to open it, and throw a flare inside. It was a simple gadget, with an iron base, a copper top, equipped with balled cotton soaked in kerosene. It exploded and a portion of it struck Dr. Samuel on the right side of the head; another portion struck Zerelda a few inches above the wrist, shattering all that part of her arm and another portion struck her young son, Archie. He died three days later.

The detectives withdrew. The bitter irony of the tragedy was that Frank and Jesse were several hundred miles away.

Public sentiment instigated a national hatred for the Pinkertons and an outpouring of sympathy for the James. Newspapers all over the country carried the story of the attack and expressed the general indignation and condemnation of the outrage. The Missouri Legislature deliberated the bombing issue and endorsed a bill that would grant Frank and Jesse amnesty for their crimes if they would voluntarily turn themselves in and stand trial for crimes allegedly committed by them during the war. The bill failed by an overwhelming majority.

This, however, did not upset Frank James' plans for marriage. In June 1874, he eloped with Annie Ralston. Miss Ralston's parents did not learn the identity of their son-in-law until several months afterward. Two months earlier Jesse had married his cousin, Zee Mimms.

The beginning of the end occurred in 1876 when what should have been a routine bank robbery in Northfield, Minnesota, turned out to be their most devastating defeat. They had begun to grow careless. The gang picked for the raid consisted of Frank and Jesse; Cole, Jim and Bob Younger; and three lesser bandits—Bill Chadwell, Charlie Pitts, and Clel Miller. The citizens of Northfield showed a rare determination. If the James gang wanted a fight they would have one. The gang was blasted to pieces with only Frank and Jesse escaping.

After Northfield, Jesse and Frank headed for Tennessee. Here they assumed new identities and lived quietly in Nashville for three years. However, their careers as railway robbers were not over.

On 15 July 1881, Jesse and Frank robbed the Chicago, Rock Island, and Pacific Railroad near Winston, Missouri, to the tune of $35,000. It was the slaying of a passenger and the conductor, that turned the nation's sympathy for the Jameses into a clamor for their arrest.

Rumors began circulating that the newly-elected governor of Missouri, Thomas T. Crittenden, had accepted the latest outlaw challenge. In his message to the legislature, he stated "three well-defined purposes and plans. First, the building and establishment of the financial security of the state; second, a broader and far-reaching system of education for our children; and third, a solemn determination to overthrow and to destroy outlawry in this state whose head and front is the James gang."

After the Winston robbery, he summoned representatives of Missouri's railroad companies to the state's capitol, Jefferson City, to discuss a reward offer for the capture of Frank and Jesse James, as the State could only offer $300 for the apprehension of a criminal. He stated they were the greatest sufferers as the "traveling public avoided the state, especially the Eastern tourists, because it was known as the 'Robber State'." Later he called the press into his office.

"A reward of $10,000 for the capture and conviction of Frank and Jesse James," had been posted, he told reporters. It was agreed that the railroads would finance the remuneration.

Originally, Frank and Jesse had ridden with a gang that would never have contemplated turning the tables on them. First, they had been shielded by their most dependable ally, the Youngers. Second, all their associates were indebted to them through the guerrilla years and were life-long inhabitants of the community in which they resided. Living would no longer be plausible should one betray the brothers, as their kinfolk would have resolved the situation. Now the new followers owed no particular allegiance; but it remained for Charles and Robert Ford to commit the conclusive piece of treachery. They owed no homage to Jesse and on several occasions openly criticized and flaunted him. The reward merely gave them an additional grievance to eliminate a man they personally loathed.

No one can be definite about the arrangements, but Bob Ford met incognito with Governor Crittenden, Clay County Sheriff James

H. Timberlake, and Kansas City Police Commissioner Henry H. Craig at the St. James Hotel in Kansas City. Ford did advance a proposition:

> If the $10,000 reward on Jesse would be inclusive for either his death or capture, Ford and his brother would pursue him, provided that the State would exonerate them of past transgressions of the law.

For the remainder of his life, Crittenden was adamant that "he had no excuses to make, no apologies to render to any living man for the part he played in this bloody drama," but denied he made a deal with Bob Ford. In sworn testimony at the coroner's inquest, Ford testified that:

> Governor Crittenden asked me if I thought I could catch Jesse and I answered yes...The governor therefore agreed to pay $10,000 apiece for the production of Jesse and Frank James, either one or the other, whether dead or alive.

Shortly after breakfast, on the morning of 3 April 1882, a gunshot was heard in the modest cottage in St. Joseph, where Jesse was living with his family, under the pseudonym of Thomas Howard. The reported slaying spread like wildfire through the city, and the streets were crowded with excited citizens eager to seek a view of the deceased.

Two days later, a special train provided by the Hannibal and St. Joseph Railroad left, with Zerelda and Zee, to take the body to Kearney. Jesse lay in state for four hours in front of the Kearney hotel; hundreds of old acquaintances, friends of the family, and curious seekers viewed the body. More than one was heard to whisper: "Is that him? Why I used to see him riding down the street!"

Afterwards the body was taken to the Samuel home and interred. Later a white marble stone was erected over his grave, with this inscription:

In loving remembrance
JESSE W. JAMES
aged 34 years, 6 months, 28 days
murdered by a traitor and coward
whose name is not worthy
to appear here

A feeling of deep reluctance to damn Jesse, let alone indict him for his many crimes, swept over the nation in a wave of revulsion at the cowardly manner in which he had been murdered. It was hard to believe that he was dead! No, it was impossible that he could die—not Jesse James! How could the public's cherished illusions be dispelled? Newspapers across the country announced the event with eight column headlines of GOOD-BYE JESSE and JESSE, BY JEHOVAH. But R. T. Bradley, in *The Outlaws of the Border or the Lives of Frank and Jesse James*, aptly summed up the nation's overall insight for him with the eulogy:

In men whom men condemn as ill
I find so much goodness still;
In men whom men deem half-divine
I find so much of sin and blot;
I hesitate to draw the line
Between the two—where God has not.

Bob Ford enjoyed a brief theatrical career, touring the country in a vaudeville show called *How I Killed Jesse James*. The act received considerable attention in the East, but throughout the Midwest and West, he was booed and tossed off the stage. No matter where he went, the stigma attached to his name could not be escaped. Ford opened a saloon in Creede, Colorado and one night, Ed Kelley, a distant relative of the Younger brothers, walked in, pointed a shotgun at him, and said, "This one's for Jesse," and pulled the trigger. The court found him guilty and sentenced him to the Colorado penitentiary for twenty years. Meanwhile Charlie, plagued with ill-health and bogged down by the opprobrium attached to his name, got drunk one night and committed suicide.

After Jesse's death, Frank James, accompanied by Major John N. Edwards, surrendered to Governor Crittenden and proclaimed solemnly, "I deliver myself to you and the law." He was assured protection and a fair trial. He was acquitted of all charges.

A free man again, Frank tried many jobs over the next three decades. He lived frugally, not by choice but by necessity, as he tried his hand at various occupations: starter at the Springfield race track, performing in a Wild West Show, farming, and on one occasion, as a shoe salesman. He died of a heart attack on 18 February 1915.

Dramatizations of events in the life of Jesse James, and of incidents pertaining to members of his gang, including the Fords, dated from immediately after the day "that dirty little coward shot Mister Howard." They continued to be stand-bys for traveling stock companies until the early 1920's, when motion pictures brought decline to these groups.

It was not until 1939 that the Twentieth Century-Fox Film Corporation brought to the screen the cinema classic on Jesse James. The attempt to exonerate Jesse somewhat for his life of banditry which had once incited such a fierce public outcry proved a box-office hit and resulted in a sequel, *The Return of Frank James.*

It all started when Nunnally Johnson, screenwriter, obtained copies of the Sedalia, Missouri, *Gazette*, which featured a series of editorials by Major John N. Edwards, who, writing at the time of the James boys, defended their criminal escapades. These articles developed the "they-drove-us-to-it" theme and depicted Frank and Jesse as valiant knights forced to a life of crime by unforgiving "blue-bellied Yankees."

Johnson wrote a screenplay partly from these articles, partly from books on Jesse James, partly from the files of the Pinkerton Detective Agency, and partly from a play called *The Purple Mask.* According to his script, the racketeers who preceded the railroad into Sedalia, Missouri, to swindle farmers out of their property, accidentally killed the James boys' mother. Jesse, a law-abiding farmer, more than evened the score with a smoking six-shooter and took to the hills. The rest of his career—the formation of the James gang and its daring raids, Jesse's suspenseful jail break with the aid of his brother, his almost nonexistent married life, and his assassination on the eve of his reform—was equally fanciful as biography, but immensely effective as melodrama. He told Darryl Zanuck, studio head, about all of this and persuaded him to delineate the life of Jesse James on the screen over the objection of the New York office.

Knowledge did not make the task of presenting the actual or legendary truth easier. The legendary won out, simply because it was stronger. "And that," as Henry King, director, said, "was fair enough. After all, the actual Jesse died more than ninety years ago—the legend of Jesse James is stronger than ever. Without maligning the dead, we tried to do justice to the living."

Johnson summed up Jesse's character, in a studio publicity release, as "a man who was neither all bad nor all good; bitter with

25

cause, kind to those he loved and dangerous to those he hated."
Zanuck was so elated with his interpretation that he remarked:

> With the picture based on these findings, it will be the most
> comprehensive on the most colorful outlaw that ever lived.
> We will not glorify him, nor picture him as entirely bad...We
> will attempt instead, to trace the psychological causes that
> led him into train and bank robbing, and to depict with
> historical accuracy the most famous of his exploits...and try
> to respect the judgment of historians and at the same time,
> keep in mind what those people who were sworn friends
> thought of him. Above all, it will show him as exactly as he
> lived.

But the producers had their reasons for their choice, quite apart
from the fact that people would rather see the myth, than the real
man. King explained that:

> Naturally, we knew quite a lot more about Jesse James than
> we put into the picture...But what we were trying to do was
> to create a Jesse James who would be worthy of the legend;
> for we knew that no matter what we or any other creators of
> fiction did now, the legend would persist. Our efforts were to
> make the legend a better one, morally as well as dra-
> matically. If we succeed it was well worth the effort.

Even today the myths linger on, mingled with history.
Throughout Jesse James country there are signs noting places where
the brothers rode, robbed or killed. To understand these feelings, con-
sider people, frustrated by the struggle of the times and unsatisfied by
routine, trying to find satisfaction and thrills in the adventures of this
desperado. Alleged immortality of the flesh has always been one of
the best tests of immortality in legend. Robin Hood still haunts Sher-
wood Forest, and Jesse James still rides the Missouri roads.

II

SITE

Pineville was the logical site for **Jesse James** *because it had personality, a rustic look, and almost perfectly resembled the James' hometown of Liberty in northern Missouri.*

Henry King worked more years, and made more pictures for Darryl Zanuck than any other director. He was at Fox even before Zanuck, joining the company in 1930 to direct Will Rogers in *Lightnin'*, remaining through the merger with Twentieth Century, and lingering to direct many of Zanuck's personal productions. The results were such smashing box-office hits as *The Country Doctor, Alexander's Ragtime Band, In Old Chicago,* and *Lloyds of London,* which vaulted Tyrone Power into overnight stardom; however, King was not Zanuck's original choice for *Jesse James.* "Zanuck did not want me," said King, "He had something else he wanted me to do. Well that script was not ready to be shot and so he finally said 'Go ahead.' "

Long tedious hours of discussion followed between Zanuck, King, and Nunnally Johnson to determine the method of handling the picture, the location for filming, and the cast to appear in it. Out of this discussion came two vitally important questions: first, should the film be shot on location in the Ozark mountain region where Jesse James lived, and second, should the entire picture be filmed in technicolor? Both were definitely answered yes.

King, flying his own Waco cabin plane, began to search for the ideal location site by going to Kearney, Missouri, where he spent considerable time questioning old mountain folk who knew the James boys, and visiting Robert James, Frank James's son. "We sat under a cherry tree and talked," reminisced King, "and I found out a lot of firsthand intimate details about the desperado, his gang, and their daring, blood-chilling exploits which had never been written down. I brought it back to Nunnually, and he incorporated as much as he could into the final shooting script."

King was aware that the countryside around Kearney and Liberty had become so modernized that it no longer resembled the rural landscape of Jesse's time. He set out to find a suitable location.

After three weeks and 15,000 miles, King was becoming discouraged. A friend, Billy Parker, an executive of the Phillips Petroleum Company, told King, "if you want to see a little town which is as America once was then go see Pineville, Missouri."

King took his friend's advice and along with assistant director

Robert Webb they flew to the southwest corner of Missouri. From the air, it became apparent that the countryside did come close to resembling the era of the James brothers. After landing they rented an automobile, and began to prowl the back roads searching for the perfect location.

After King and Webb arrived in Pineville, they inquired of a local resident whom they should see about using the community for the location of a movie. Bewildered, the man told them to see Mayor F. T. Drumm, who according to King, "was at that moment mowing the grass on the courthouse lawn."

After the purpose of their visit was explained, Mayor Drumm was asked to assemble together all the city and county civic leaders for a dinner, to be hosted by King. Here King explained that Pineville was the logical site for *Jesse James* because it had personality, a rustic look, and almost perfectly resembled the James' hometown of Liberty in northern Missouri. He also believed the scenery, the big caves, crystal clear streams, and sheer bluffs were perfect background for the essential gun battles and horseback leaps. It was this that tempted the studio to seek out the site for the filming of the picture.

King outlined the cost of making such a picture, the vast money to be expended for remodeling the region to resemble the 1880's, fixtures, hiring local labor, extras, transportation of actors and crew back and forth from Hollywood. He went on to add that in the event the decision was made to film in the area the entire cast would be brought. "When you take all that in consideration, I think it will cost upward of $20,000," said King, "to do just the work to prepare what we aim to do."

In closing, King informed those present "that before preparations could begin, I must present before the Board of Directors and the budget committee what it will cost to operate each day in Pineville, and exactly what it will cost to make these operations from the time we leave Hollywood until we finish here and return to Hollywood!"

Many residents left the meeting skeptical, because of bitter experiences with "city slicker" promoters, and told local townspeople and tourists that "it was just another promotion scheme." For weeks there had been talk, TALK, TALK, about what was going to happen in Pineville when "they" would make the movie. But most of the townfolk went around with their "tongues in cheeks," until Mayor

Drumm received a telegram from Henry King telling him to go ahead with advance arrangements, confirming "that the decision was rendered in favor of doing the picture in Pineville...and you can acquaint those in the vicinity with these facts." Within a matter of minutes you could have knocked over with one feather the collective citizenry of Pineville when they heard the movie personnel were heading in. Virtually every individual in the town joined the whirlpool of activity and excitement, engrossed upon personal plans and ambitions. Almost the whole town went 'plum crazy', but there were a few like Lump Ward, the town disgrace who felt it would ruin the community. "I never liked movies anyhow," he said, "and they're all lousy and this proves it and the hell with them."

It was like hearing that Ringling Brothers Circus was coming to town. The president of the Pineville Chamber of Commerce enthusiastically declared, "It's the biggest thing that ever happened to us, and we're proud that a great many folks will have the opportunity of at least seeing movies of the beauty of our Ozark scenery." Even if the President of the United States had announced his intentions to speak on one of his transcontinental tours, it could not have created more excitement. "We are happy to have Hollywood with us," said Mayor Drumm, "because someone like them can see the natural beauty of our land of a Million Smiles; happy because we know they are going to obey our slogan while in the Ozarks, 'Keep Smiling.' "

The movie created so much furor that there was even a suggestion to change the town's name to Hollywoodville. The idea was dropped, as many thought it was going *too far* and might be regretted in later years. "Bring on your World's Fairs!" cried Pineville. "Bring on your little location trips to San Fernando Valley!" cried the Hollywood contingent. There was a certain proud scorn in both cries; it was an incredible windfall, the like of which would not come again.

Overcome with such exuberance, the Mayor almost wore out the telegram by taking it out of his hip pocket to read to friends he met on the street. Even the local newspapers ran a copy of it on their front page; and even before the day was over, it became an item in newspapers all over the country.

The state of Missouri took notice of the unusual affair. Governor Lloyd Stark wired King, "I am delighted and proud that you have chosen Missouri for the filming of the *Jesse James* picture. I welcome

31

you and your associates to our state...."

Governor Stark received an acknowledgment from King. It said, in part, "I want to thank you very much in behalf of our Twentieth Century-Fox troupe for your telegram of welcome...the hospitality and cooperation of your people has been gratifying...but we all will be disappointed unless you, too, can be my guest on the set while we are in your charming state...."

Later an invitation was dispatched to the movie troupe by Governor Stark and other elected officials to visit Missouri's State Capitol and to see for themselves the interpretation of a Jesse James holdup in the Thomas Hart Benton mural. The visit never materialized and one young lady was quite upset saying, "I was promised a personal introduction to them by my boss."

The Pineville City Council went into special session to talk about the expected parking problem, establishment of screened, outdoor eating places to accommodate visitors, and a thousand other details necessary to the preparations for the great event. Even the Chamber of Commerce took action by announcing that the annual McDonald County Fair, one of the district's traditional celebrations, would be cancelled because its scheduled dates might interfere with the operations of the film company. Both organizations wanted to facilitate the fullest cooperation with King.

Suddenly, and almost without warning, local townspeople launched one of the most intensive cleanup campaigns in their community's history. They raked leaves, picked up loose debris, mowed their lawns, and, in some instances, even installed modern plumbing. Housewives started their fall house cleaning a month ahead of time, and many families volunteered to move out of their homes, bag and baggage, if the movie company needed additional accommodations. Those families that kept extras, and technicians, were paid one dollar a day per person and were expected to provide them sleeping space and feed them three times a day. "And they had an appetite," said one lady.

In the neighboring resort town of Noel the excitement reached a similar fervor. Only a few weeks before, resort owners and cafes were enjoying a fair degree of business, and cars bearing licenses from far-away states attracted little attention. Then, the placid scene changed, and the area turned into a state of confusion. A few phonies drifted

32

Jesse James, Nebraska City, Nebraska, 1875.

The James Home Near Kearney, Missouri, in the 1880's.

PROCLAMATION

OF THE

GOVERNOR OF MISSOURI!

REWARDS

FOR THE ARREST OF

Express and Train Robbers.

STATE OF MISSOURI,
EXECUTIVE DEPARTMENT.

WHEREAS, It has been made known to me, as the Governor of the State of Missouri, that certain parties, whose names are to me unknown, have confederated and banded themselves together for the purpose of committing robberies and other depredations within this State ; and

WHEREAS, Said parties did, on or about the Eighth day of October, 1879, stop a train near Glendale, in the county of Jackson, in said State, and, with force and violence, take, steal and carry away the money and other express matter being carried thereon ; and

WHEREAS, On the fifteenth day of July 1881, said parties and their confederates did stop a train upon the line of the Chicago, Rock Island and Pacific Railroad, near Winston, in the County of Daviess, in said State, and, with force and violence, take, steal, and carry away the money and other express matter being carried thereon ; and, in perpetration of the robbery last aforesaid, the parties engaged therein did kill and murder one WILLIAM WESTFALL, the conductor of the train, together with one JOHN McCULLOCH, who was at the time in the employ of said company, then on said train ; and

WHEREAS, FRANK JAMES and JESSE W. JAMES stand indicted in the Circuit Court of said Daviess County, for the murder of JOHN W. SHEETS, and the parties engaged in the robberies and murders aforesaid have fled from justice and have absconded and secreted themselves :

NOW, THEREFORE, in consideration of the premises, and in lieu of all other rewards heretofore offered for the arrest or conviction of the parties aforesaid, or either of them, by any person or corporation, I, THOMAS T. CRITTENDEN, Governor of the State of Missouri, do hereby offer a reward of five thousand dollars ($5,000.00) for the arrest and conviction of each person participating in either of the robberies or murders aforesaid, excepting the said FRANK JAMES and JESSE W. JAMES ; and for the arrest and delivery of said

FRANK JAMES and JESSE W. JAMES,

and each or either of them, to the sheriff of said Daviess County, I hereby offer a reward of five thousand dollars, ($5,000.00,) and for the conviction of either of the parties last aforesaid of participation in either of the murders or robberies above mentioned, I hereby offer a further reward of five thousand dollars, ($5,000.00.)

IN TESTIMONY WHEREOF, I have hereunto set my hand and caused to be affixed the Great Seal of the State of Missouri. Done

[SEAL.]   at the City of Jefferson on this 28th day of July, A. D. 1881

THOS. T. CRITTENDEN.

By the Governor :

MICH'L K. McGRATH, Sec'y of State.

Reward Proclamation Issued by Governor Crittenden

Jesse James Shot by Robert Ford.

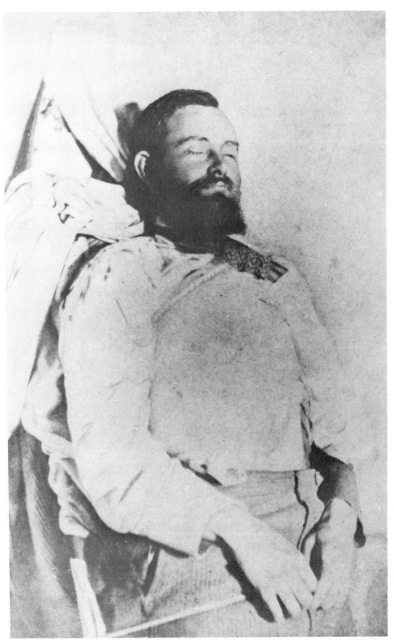

Jesse in Death.

Do you know that

JESSE JAMES

---was such a daring desperado that he and his brother Frank gave to an entire decade of American history the title of the "Serious Seventies." Their native Missouri became known as the "Robber State." The artist's sketch shows Tyrone Power and Henry Fonda in the starring roles of Jesse and Frank James in the 20th Century-Fox Technicolor production "Jesse James."

--~ pursued the longest continuous career of banditry in this country-- 16 years, from 1866 to 1882.

---had many friends throughout the Missouri hills who never referred to him as an outlaw. "Horse and revolver work" was their version of Jesse's activities!

--- invented bank robbery and was the first to hold up a railroad train. Passengers were so curious about this new "experience" that they calmly asked the outlaws to explain in detail what it was all about.

--- was a strange inexplicable mixture of good and bad, who became a conscientious church member in the midst of his outlaw career.

Odd Facts Feature.

Tyrone Power as Jesse James.

Henry King rehearsing a scene with Nancy Kelly, Tyrone Power.

Tyrone Power

Henry Fonda and Tyrone Power "horse around" between takes.

Tyrone Power and crew prepare for train robbing sequence.

Reward poster used in *Jesse James*

For Realism, Director King wanted dirt around the square.
And he got it—six inches of dirt, over streets recently paved.

Hollywood technicians were working to transform Pineville
into an unreal town of the 1880's.

The locomotive used to depict the St. Louis Midland R.R.

Henry King filming the opening scene for the movie. Scene discarded during editing.

An estimated 4,000 to 5,000 persons lined the railroad tracks at Noel awaiting the arrival of the train bearing cast and crew.

The curious, some sixteen thousand daily, flocked to Noel and Pineville, eager to see the film stars.

Workmen, camera crew, extras, and spectators are shown watching Henry Fonda, as Frank James, being brought to the Liberty courthouse and jail by soldiers and sheriff's deputies.

Workmen and camera crew prepare to film the surrender of Jesse to Marshal Will Wright.

Henry Fonda, Tyrone Power

Tyrone Power, Henry Fonda

in, but mostly the crowds were made up of respectable families who wanted to see the fun and have a little part in it. As one woman said, "It's a bonanza. It's like the gold rush to Alaska!"

"Let Pineville have the movie set," said the people of Noel "just as long as the crowds come here to see the stars." Henry King showed a bit of diplomacy when he established his headquarters in Noel, as the two rival communities had a long-standing feud, which at times had threatened to assume proportions similar to those family affairs in the hills of Tennessee.

"It'll hurt Pineville more'n it'll help it," Lump Ward declared gloomily. "Messin' up the town, stirrin' up a lot of unrest, and all we'll get out of it is a little sandwich money from the tourists. The movie folks are all going to stay over at the hotel. Take it from me, Noel is the real Jesse James in this show. They're getting most of the money and a lot of the publicity, but we've got swimmin' holes out here on Big Sugar that makes theirs look like mud puddles."

Fortunately the towns had "shook hands," so to speak, and all was forgotten, at least for the time being. The movie company reserved the only tourist hotel, several private homes, and a number of cabins, cottages, trailers, and whatever else could be used for accommodations for their personnel. Townspeople admitted that the lodgings were not "anything fancy," but at least they were clean, comfortable, and "strictly modern." There was one exception as someone had forgotten to install plumbing in the cottage occupied by Jane Darwell. Upon her arrival, she discovered that the only toilet available was an outhouse some distance from the cabin. She made her way there, but was spied by a small youngster who was determined to take her picture. He made his way to the outhouse, flung the door open and quickly shot Jane's photograph as she sat there.

"The folks opened their houses for us," remarked Jim Denton, the studio's chief publicist. "They just thought it was the kindly thing to do. I stayed in the house of the lumber merchant. His wife had to be argued with before she'd take six dollars a week." However, instead of trying to raise prices and "trim" the Hollywood people, the natives treated the film troupe more as their guests than someone to fleece.

Three of Noel's eating establishments were selected for use of the company's cast and crew. New equipment was installed and one owner reported he had imported some "high-powered cooks" for the occasion. Chicken, steak, and trout dinners sold for fifty cents and other items on the menu were comparably priced.

Business began to soar when tourists, already vacationing in the area, began to make arrangements to extend their visits. Inquiries from prospective visitors poured in by the thousands, which necessitated the recreation and business places remaining open at least a month after the scheduled summer season's closing date. Ordinarily reserved, these southwest Missourians went Hollywood in a conspicuous way.

Supplies of colored sunglasses were exhausted and each stranger in the community was accepted as being from Hollywood. Adding to the general confusion, the Hollywood people thought the tourists were natives, and the natives thought the tourists were movie folks and asked them for jobs.

Over at the drugstore, which was doing a booming soft drink business, a young lady thought Jesse himself had arrived when a be-whiskered man in overalls and a slouch hat reeled in and, taking hold of her bobbed hair and giving it a good stout yank, said, "How're you doin', kid?" From a peaceful little town where nothing ever happened, Pineville had suddenly became a town where anything might happen.

A quiet-mannered man, sitting in a chair in the shade of a building, was approached by a group of tourists and bombarded with questions about what the town would do with its unexpected windfall. "Make some improvements?" suggested a lady in the group, to which the man replied, he supposed so. "What's the population of this place anyway?" someone finally asked. The quiet-mannered man chuckled. "That's what I'd like to know," he answered. "I'm a painter from Hollywood."

The labor question was the subject of discussion. It seems a couple of union organizers had come in and were trying to sign up the local job seekers on a ninety cent per hour platform. Some were "fer" and others "agin," but all decided to take what the movie company elected to pay.

Sentiment in Pineville ranged all the way from high enthusiasm to downright pessimism. Even with the painter from Hollywood assuring the crowd that "this will bring at least a hundred thousand dollars into this section of the country," a local grocer refused to get excited.

Pineville, however, was concerned with an ethical evaluation of the outlaw's career. The citizenery was interested in enjoying to the fullest the break in the small town monotony which came from being chosen as the scene of a motion picture. Glamour and adventure were in the air. Olympus had moved to Pineville, and the natives were feasting on nectar and ambrosia.

One of the first arrivals in the region was Sidney Bowen, studio financial manager. Setting up offices at Pineville and at Noel, it was his job to manage the mass of details coincident with preparations for the filming, and to contact residents, property owners, and merchants and secure all necessary location sites and housing facilities.

Accompanying Bowen was Thomas Pryor, who, as paymaster, supervised the finances, and set up offices in both Pineville and Noel. Extras and drivers received $2.50 per day, owners of horses were paid a dollar a day, and if a vehicle was used, another fifty cents was received. Overall the venture was quite profitable.

King had announced that he expected to use at least one-half of Pineville's population as extras in the picture. He had laid down the ultimatum, however, that all men who hoped for such jobs must have beards. "They'll look more like men did during Jesse James' time," Mayor Drumm said, "and even if they don't get to be extras in the picture, they'll create an atmosphere and generate a lot of valuable publicity."

There was scarely a man, woman or child, who wasn't experiencing the thrill of a lifetime in anticipation of being one of the extras. Some needed the money, others just wanted to be in the "moving pic'ure." Almost everybody who wanted to be in the movies was given some type of part, but King refused to give the barber a job, as he was the only one in town, and the actors needed a shave.

One lady, who refused to part with a stylish bob, planned to wear an old-fashioned "slat-bonnet" to cover her hair. "I've already got my horse and sidesaddle," she said. "One of my neighbors has a white Arabian I'd like to ride, but I expect it would cause trouble, that horse is too nervous to act in a picture."

Among the many natives who were given extra work was an eighteen-year-old mountain girl. She worked only two days, but when she appeared at the pay booth to collect her salary, she was obviously excited. "At last I've got mah life ambition," she announced. "I've

35

earned enough to set mahself up in business!"

"What kind of business?" demanded Pryor, in amazement.

"Well," she said, "now I can buy two pigs and staht raisn' moah pigs!"

One little boy who played in two local scenes, stated emphatically he had no desire to go to Hollywood. "The movie company came in here when most of us were in need of ready cash," he said, "but I'm going to be a deep-sea diver" as he laconically stuck a dollar bill in a letter and mailed it to his mother.

Money started flowing in a gentle stream and practically every local inhabitant, off relief, kept feeling in their pockets to see if it wasn't a dream. "Imagine," replied one lady, "making four dollars a day, when the going pay was just a dollar! My husband drove his truck and earned thirteen dollars a day. We purchased our first washing machine with cash."

The atmosphere of Pineville had become slightly crazy. One farmer hitched up his team and drove into town. No sooner had he arrived than an assistant director shouted to him, "get your horse over there with the rest of the extras." As the farmer started to object, he found himself surrounded by a group of autograph seekers. A friend hailed the farmer shortly afterwards as he saw him start to leave town.

"Where you goin' in such a hurry," he said.

"Back to the farm. The whole town's gone plumb crazy," the farmer shouted.

Hollywood technicians were transforming dowdy and innocent Pineville into an unreal town of the 1880's. The Dixie Belle Saloon had gone up, so had the sheriff's headquarters, and the Liberty *Weekly Gazette*. Power lines had been removed. King had the technicians take three thousand truck and wagon loads of dirt and gravel and pour it over the anachronistic concrete. Lump Ward told the boys on the corner that the town was doomed; however, one councilman felt relieved as he said, "I'm sorry we put the concrete in. It makes the city too damn hot."

The deputy sheriff, sitting on the curb in front of the courthouse proved a ready spokesman as he watched the trucks as they drove up in his jailyard. "This is going to do a lot for Pineville," he smiled, "put us on the map. See that lot over there with the pile of gravel on it? That's my lot, and I was going to put up a building on it, but the movie people are doing it for me.''

The technicians placed false fronts and wooden awnings on existing buildings that gave them an aged appearance by the use of paints and stains which would lend itself to the technicolor process, and paneled plate glass windows with strips to represent small window panes. Old fashioned street lighting fixtures were arranged on the walls of business fronts and on posts around the square. A sign chalked on the board in front of the store read as follows: ''Coon skins, 35 cents; Beef, 2½ cents lb.'' Even the courthouse got a picturesque appearance with a stone plaque over the entrance inscribed, ''Clay County Courthouse.'' Constructed on the lawn were hitching racks, deeply worn as if long used, an old well, and water troughs which came in handy as farmers took advantage of them to water their livestock being used for the picture. All this was too much for the natives. They would just sit on the curbstone and gape. Many of the tourists refused to believe that the public square was actually part of the town and not a motion picture set. ''Where,'' asked one of the tourists, ''will all you people go when the movie studio tears down the buildings?''

III

PREPARATIONS

Many of the national news magazines featured special layouts on the film. **Life** *sent in photographer Alfred Eisenstadt along with a writer to do a photo essay...*

Fortunately, Twentieth Century-Fox had under contract the perfect actor to play Jesse James. Darryl Zanuck told how his choice of a leading man for *Sing, Baby, Sing* a couple of years before was yielded to by the protests of director Sidney Lanfield.

"He was a new young player in whom I had great confidence," said Zanuck. But after a day or two of shooting, Lanfield was still dissatisfied, and the actor was taken from the cast. Asked to name the actor, Zanuck answered "Tyrone Power."

Henry Forda was selected to portray Frank James. Walter Brennan was scheduled to depict Major Rufus Cobb, but at the last moment Henry Hull substituted. Nancy Kelly was given the feminine romantic lead of Zee. Randolph Scott was assigned to play Will Wright, the United States Marshal. A call to "central casting" produced some powerful-looking characters which included Slim Summerville, J. Edward Bromberg, Brian Donlevy, John Carradine, Donald Meek, Johnnie Russell, Lon Chaney, Jr., Jane Darwell, Harold Goodwin, George Breakston, Charles Tannen and Ernest Whitman.

Before King and his *Jesse James* company left Hollywood, Harry Brand, studio publicist, arranged to have a coast-to-coast radio broadcast with not only the stars, but people who knew the James boys. It would be one of several pre-release exploitation stunts to create increasing interest in the film.

Announcer: (Dramatically) During the period of America's westward march when the Iron Horse was helping to push the frontier toward the setting sun, colorful personalities, both good and evil, sprang into national prominence. It was this turbulent and lawless era that produced the most famous outlaw that ever lived!

Voice: Wanted, dead or alive, the outlaw Jesse James!

Voice: Robber...Killer! He must hang!

Voice: This country is under martial law pending the trial of the outlaw, Jesse James!

Announcer: Jesse James! A name that once struck fear over a thousand miles of borderland! Yet as many cheered him as feared him and to the simple folks who knew he was a victim of cruel injustice...one gentle girl loved him...and his life was the epic story of a lawless era!

It is the spectacular drama of this outlaw's life that brings Darryl Zanuck and Twentieth Century-Fox to portray it on the screen in marvelous technicolor. It will be coming to this area soon.

Newspapers all over the country were beginning to show unusual interest in the film by assigning staff and feature writers to cover the production. The clamor for special stories and "art" on the film was such that Brand sent reinforcements from the studio publicity department on location.

Many of the national news magazines featured special layouts on the film. *Life* sent in photographer Alfred Eisenstadt along with a writer to do a photo essay. Jimmy Starr, Hollywood columnist, accompanied by his wife, made a special trip to the area seeking material, and even Louella Parsons asked for a 300 word skeletonized keyhole portrait on Donald Meek.

The demand for "exclusive" material was extraordinary and guidelines were set up by Brand on how to write a story.

Each story should have what we call "credits" in it: name of film, director Henry King, 20th Century-Fox, and as many of stars names as you can use gracefully without making the story smell; when the copy runs more than two pages the title of the film should be in the story twice. Always try, of course, to bring in the credits in as logical and essential way possible so the copy desk of newspapers won't be tempted too much to cut it out.

In mentioning the players, they should be mentioned in order of billing importance (which has a lot of crap to do with contracts and whatnot) Tyrone Power, Henry Fonda, Nancy

Kelly, Randolph Scott, Jane Darwell, etc. in this order.

Double space all copy, starting a quarter down the page about, without any marking at top of page, no name or by-line.

We gotta sell this show in the copy not just the life of Jesse James, but as a historical technicolor film of the march of civilization westward, etc. That's the general idea anyway.

King and Power arrived several days in advance of the train by private plane. They admitted that there was a time on their flight from Burbank, California when they would rather have been on the ground. "We were flying over a mountain at an elevation of about 14,000 feet, and it was so bumpy we both became nauseated," Power recounted. "King told me maybe I would feel better if I ate something. I found a sandwich, and then happened to notice it was thickly buttered. Then I really did get ill. I finally ended up by drinking soda pop."

Power said there was nothing in his contract to prevent his flying a plane, but Twentieth Century-Fox "would just as soon I didn't." He signed autographs and answered questions about the picture and was sincerely enthusiastic about the role he was going to play. "I regard this as one of the most important roles I have ever played," he told reporters.

"Ever since I began my acting career I have always wanted to appear in a production based upon the life of a real person," Power pointed out. "I had that opportunity in *Marie Antoinette,* and now in my role as Jesse James I try to imagine how he would have talked or acted, and what his reactions would have been when confronted with the many perils which marked his life. I believe the fact that I am portraying the life of a real man tends to lend a certain sincerity to my acting which I might otherwise not have in a fictional role."

There were many who believed the young star's performance in the film would turn out to be the greatest of his triumphal career. Power, who modestly declined to comment, pointed out that his present role was different than any he had ever tried before.

He was enthusiastic over the possibilities of such a region as the

Ozarks for future technicolor productions. "The setting is perfect," he told his newly-made friends, "and the scenery is beautiful."

Here and there, the movie company and the Ozark people did not quite see eye to eye. There was the splendidly bearded farmer who Power sought to befriend. Observing the gentleman's whiskers with envy and amazement, Power got into a conversation with him, and learned that he wished to appear before the cameras, but somehow, when he applied for extra work, he had been overlooked.

Power promised to fix that up. He introduced the farmer to King, who agreed to give him a part. Later Power was surprised to find the farmer tending his garden when he should have been on location. Naturally, Power asked the reason. "Hell," said the farmer. "That feller wanted me to be an orator."

Power was walking down the streets of Pineville when he was accosted by another bewhiskered native. He admitted that he was playing the role of Jesse James and the native opined "He war a skunk." Rather startled, poor Power protested, "Isn't that a matter of opinion?" The native replied, "Opinion 'round here is he war a skunk." That seemed to settle the matter.

While Power was studying his part and making new friends, King set out to see an Ozark mountaineer. He wanted to take some shots of the man, his home, and the clear stream which ran through his property.

"What are you going to use it for?" he drawled.

"We're going to shoot *Jesse James* there," replied King.

The old man scratched his beard and looked puzzled. "You don't know Jesse's been shot?"

After some discussion on the matter he persuaded the old man to rent the property and handed him a contract to sign.

"I can't write my name, but I'll put my mark on the paper," the old man explained, and affixed an "X" to the contract.

"By the way," he asked a moment later, "is that a legal document I justed signed?" He was told it was.

"Then I'll have to sign my legal name," he told them, marking another "X" opposite the original one.

King even tried to rent or buy a still that was in operation in the woods. He had been exploring the local countryside and came across some moonshiners engaged in their cheerful operation. After a friendly discussion of this and that and the movies, King suggested that he'd pay well for the still and would cart it off as soon as it cooled. Still friendly, but terribly serious, the moonshiners said, "Mister, she ain't goin' to cool off, because we ain't aimin' to shut'er down. Any objections?" There were none.

A locomotive was needed to represent equipment of the St. Louis Midland Railroad for the train sequences, and King set out to find one. He found it in Dardanelle, Arkansas. Two passenger cars and a combination passenger and express car, with the engine, made up the train. The coaches had wooden seats with green upholstery and kerosene lamps. King had it sent to Little Rock, Arkansas, so it could be overhauled, painted and equipped with new flues.

Meanwhile, King returned to supervise last minute details in the reconstruction of the Crowder farm into the Jesse James homestead. A wire fence around the yard was replaced by a picket fence and a split-rail fence was erected near the barn. Out back, a room of the Crowder house had to be duplicated, fireplace, stairway and all, to accommodate the cameras, lights and all the equipment necessary to take interior shots.

Mrs. Florence Crowder thought it was a "heap o' confusion." Robert Webb had negotiated a contract with her, and it was speculated that $3,000 was paid, however, he rented it for ten dollars a day. In addition, he hired two of her sons. "We got the farm so cheaply," he said, "I figured it wouldn't do any harm to help her make a little more. I suggested that it would be all right with us if her two sons sold a little soda pop to the hordes of people trampling over her place...."

The next thing Mrs. Crowder knew was that the place was overrun with actors and visitors with no one paying any attention to her. She often stood in one corner of the yard, looking on in bewilderment, and selling soda pop and fresh milk, charging only a nickel for it. "I didn't know what I was getting into," said Mrs. Crowder, wishing she had never signed that paper.

"What with her soda pop concession and this and that, she cleaned up several thousand dollars," said Webb. Her period of wealth, however, ended in tragedy. The excitement, or perhaps the strain of having that much money suddenly, was too much for her. Mrs. Crowder suffered a nervous breakdown caused, according to relatives, by the rabble-rousing and the continuous stream of visitors to the home. This attributed to her death by heart disease several months later.

Pineville was rapidly becoming inundated by tourists. Some came as far away as Baghdad, Iraq. Hundreds of applications for work in the picture began piling up, and letters were received from almost every part of the country. The railroads and bus lines ran excursions, and the roads were jammed with cars.

With only a dime in his pocket, a farm boy hitch-hiked almost 100 miles to Pineville. Two days later, on his return trip, he was telling about his experiences to a motorist who had picked him up. "I spent five cents for a bottle of soda pop," he explained, "and I had to milk a bunch of cows for a man before I could get anything to eat, but I've still got a nickel and I'm almost back home again."

Some people came with the curiosity of how a motion picture was made, some to take photographs, while others were awaiting the arrival of the special train bearing the cast and equipment. Most of the natives shook their heads doubtfully. "Pineville will never be the same," they said. A majority of them, with plenty of cash, probably did not care much. They were more concerned with "When are the movie people leaving?" and "Are the movie people coming back here to make another picture?"

Every night was party night. Power spent an hour or more at Shadow Lake, sitting in a roped off section. He signed autographs and was occasionally interviewed by the press. Power thought that Noel was "a cross between New York and Hollywood."

"In Hollywood you expect to work hard," explained Power, "and in New York you expect crowds of autograph hunters, but in Noel you have both to encounter."

He finally hit upon the time-saving device of signing his name simply, "Ty Power," to avoid an attack of writer's cramp.

46

The night before the train arrived the dance lasted well after midnight and many of the merrymakers spent the night on the lawn near the depot, while a few passed the time idly away. An estimated 4,000 to 5,000 persons lined the streets awaiting the arrival of the special train. A young man named Elmer, from Joplin, Missouri, saw to it that many persons got something to eat. He bought loaves of bread, cheese, and hot dogs and distributed the food to the crowd. Just why he was so generous was never explained. Many hundreds of people went without breakfast in the desire to get a glimpse of the stars.

The next morning a train whistle could be heard in the distance. The heavy-eyed crowd stirred and surged forward to the front of the station, and a locomotive pulling a freight train swished past. The crowd was disappointed, but thirty minutes later another train whistle could be heard in the distance. This time it was the special train bearing the cast and crew, comprising nearly a hundred in all. It took four full baggage cars to bring all the equipment.

King and Sidney Bowen met the train with buses and cars to take the cast and crew members to various living quarters, scattered throughout the town. The edge was taken off the situation when a dozen or more bodyguards cleared a path for the cast. "What in hell is going on here?" asked Henry Hull, when he saw several hundred persons gathered outside his train window. When he heard that a majority of persons in the crowd probably were autograph seekers, he clasped his hand across his forehead and murmured, "This is going to be awful."

Hull had been brought to play the role of Major Rufus Cobb, the newspaper editor friend of Frank and Jesse James. "King saw me in New York while I was there playing the role of Jeeter Lester in *Tobacco Road*," Hull explained. "He arrived at the conclusion that Major Cobb was a type similar to Jeeter, although more refined."

Hull said his father was, at one time, city editor on the *Louisville* (Kentucky) *Courier-Journal* and this was the first time he had ever had to essay such a role himself. "I've been reading about this editor, Cobb, and I want to say I think he's all right," Hull told reporters. "If all newspapermen today were like Cobb, there would be bigger and better newspapers."

The reporters asked the stage star for a brief story of his life, and he rummaged around in his suitcase until he found a manuscript and handed it to one of them. "Here's one I wrote all by myself," he told them. "Take it with you."

One of the first things Donald Meek did after departing the train was to purchase a flashlight to guide him along a mountain stream to the cottage where he was staying. "I have no desire to be fed to the fish as yet," he explained.

Brian Donlevy bounced off the train, attired in a white sailor suit with cap to match. He later had to discard it as he discovered it enabled autograph seekers to spot him at least two blocks away. Jane Darwell wore a simple light black and white figured dress and black straw hat. With a dapper tilt to his Panama hat, John Carradine arrived for the sole purpose, he explained, of killing Jesse James. Natives thought he was talking in a foreign tongue until they discovered he was only indulging in his favorite occupation—reciting lines from Shakespeare. When Carradine stepped from the train platform he was surrounded by autograph seekers. A friend sought to rescue him, but he waved him aside. "Leave them alone," he smiled. "If the autograph seekers didn't come around I'd think I was slipping."

The cast emerged on the side opposite the crowd, entered the station, jumped out the window and proceeded to enter the waiting vehicles. Officials reported it was done to avoid confusion. Once they were situated, guards were posted around their living quarters to protect their privacy.

Women tourists almost started a stampede when Power and Fonda arrived at a Noel cafe for their breakfast. Although attempts were made to provide the stars privacy, admirers showed ingenuity in methods of crashing the gate. Singling out a girl in the crowd, Fonda called to her: "Young lady, do you know what I'm going to do sometime? I'm going over to your house and watch you eat breakfast."

The same attitude existed later that day at Shadow Lake where an orchestra was playing. The dance floor was comfortably crowded, but the dancers did not have their hearts in it—not the girls anyway. They kept looking at the door.

For all their vigil, however, Jane Darwell, Randolph Scott, and several minor members of the troupe, walked through the dance to a table on a porch overlooking the river and started eating before anyone saw them. Upon being observed, there was a small rush for autographs from Scott and Miss Darwell, which they graciously gave out between bites. "I'm used to it," she said. Scott summed it up when he told newsmen, "We're bothered with autograph seekers in Hollywood, too, but the people here seem to be much more civil and considerate."

The girls in the crowd still kept watching the door, and all of a sudden, without any apparent signal, most of them rushed out of the place and up the street to a restaurant. They jammed, shoved, and fought their way into the place. They came to an abrupt halt at a chain hastily thrown up to bar the entrance to a sort of private dinner room. They gaped, stared and gasped.

"It's HIM kid," said a blonde from Oklahoma ecstatically.

"Where? Where is he," said another blonde from Kansas.

"Right there. At that table by the winda. Looka him. Ain't he sweet?"

"Oh, HIM. Why it's only Henry Fonda. I thought you meant it was Tyrone."

If the fact that he was playing a second fiddle to his co-worker was evident to Fonda, a tired-looking young man with crisp, dark hair, he gave no sign of it. He went on munching a ham sandwich. And if he did know how some of the girls felt about it, he may have gained some satisfaction from the fact that he had undeniably cramped Power's entrance by getting there first.

Power arrived at the restaurant a few minutes later. He was on the sidewalk in front of the little frame building before the mob recognized him. Then, in, full cry, the onlookers crowded in and Power fled to the room behind the chain. He sat down with Fonda beside a screened, opened window and ordered fried chicken, a favorite dish.

Hungry after a strenuous day of sight-seeing, he looked up in anticipation when the waitress brought in his order. On his plate were two chicken wings.

"I guess all that chicken learned how to do was fly," he commented.

When the two started to leave, they had a choice of two back doors. Half the crowd, led by a young woman with a minature camera, stationed itself at one back door. The other half, led by a woman with a box camera, covered the other door.

Like hunted animals, Power and Fonda looked out first one door and then the other. They chose the one nearest the hotel, with the valiant Donlevy running interference for them, slamming the door shut in time's proverbial nick.

Panting slightly, the stars collapsed in chairs and relaxed in the comparative quiet of a bevy of reporters and photographers, who had been summoned from the soft drink place to the hotel for their interview.

The respite was brief. The crowd surged against the windows of the room they were in and pressed its collective nose against the screen.

"Tyrone," screamed another blonde. "Look this way! Look at me!"

"Why?" asked Power, reasonably enough, but he looked anyway.

While the crowd stood guard outside, the press talked to Power, Fonda, Donlevy, Scott, Kelly, Darwell, and other minor members of the troupe and took pictures.

Power was not to be trapped into calling his temporary home in Noel a mess. "I don't think it's a mess at all," he said. "I like it. I'll admit I never saw a crowd as big as this at any place I've ever been on location. And this part of the country is a perfect setting for the story. It couldn't be better."

Power said he was enjoying "roughing it" in the rugged hill country, and had found the homespun trousers, old checkered shirt and leather boots he had to wear in the film an ideal attire for fishing trips or horseback rides.

"Those James boys had the right idea about comfortable clothing," he told them.

In a more serious mood, the young star had confided he was particularly happy over being given the coveted role of Jesse James because of the opportunity to portray on the screen the life of a real individual whose name had been a byword with every school boy of the country for years.

Fonda was just as enthusastic about playing Frank James, and said he had to learn to chew tobacco for his role in the film.

"I'm learning how to spit almost as good as the natives now," he boasted.

"The first thing I did," said Nancy Kelly, "when I went sightseeing was to purchase a pair of blue denim overalls and packed away my frilly dresses."

Miss Kelly had been learning how to speak with the soft drawling dialect of the Ozark natives. As the reporters got up to leave, she bade them goodbye, and then remarked coyly: "You all must come back h'yar and see us sometime. We'uns ud be powerful glad to see you."

By this time the crowd was solidly massed outside the hotel, and a deputy sheriff was talking about "clearing out the place." He was only talking though. The crowd was too big for one deputy, or for ten, for that matter.

As they opened the door, the crowd shouted, "Bring 'em out here. Let us see 'em."

Somebody came out and set a long table in front of the porch of the hotel. While it was being placed, a waitress from the restaurant came out carrying a tray and waving a half-smoked cigarette butt. "Looka what I get," she chortled. "It's one of Tyrone's cigarettes. He said to auction it off and I'd get forty percent and he'd get the rest."

The crowd paid no attention to her. They watched the door. And this time, watching was rewarded. Out on a table stepped Jim Denton, publicist. "Ladies and Gentlemen," he said, "Mr. Power, Mr. Fonda, Mr. Scott, Mr. Donlevy, and Miss Darwell will come outside. They will give autographs to everyone who wants them." He introduced them but by the time he got to Mr. Donlevy's introduction he was ignored by the crowd. It had swarmed over Power and Fonda. They were busy autographing.

Later that afternoon, most of the members of the company went sight-seeing, striking up acquaintances with natives and visitors. Fonda was stopped by a woman who asked him "to please stand still until I get a look at you, because I've never seen a movie star before." Fonda was embarrassed, but complied and she stared for a few minutes. When he started to walk away, she stopped him again and remarked "Just which one are you anyway?"

John Carradine became acquainted with the owner of a dance pavilion, formerly a widely known cellist. A friend chanced to over-

51

hear Carradine engaged in a learned discussion about music with the cellist.

"I didn't know you knew so much about music," he told Carradine.

"Frankly," said the actor, unperturbed, "I don't, but I've been learning how to play the piano and I'm trying to get in the mood to go back and practice again."

The natives thought Power was one of the greatest fellows it had ever been their opportunity to meet. He discussed their crops with them, spun yarns and soon became acquainted to them as an all-round regular fellow. Power said simply and sincerely, "They are the most hospitable people I have ever met."

Streams of motorists had begun to arrive early at Noel and by midmorn the streets were packed with 16,000 to 17,000 automobiles. A crowd estimated at 20,000, all eating and drinking, standing around in town, taking pictures from the roof of cars and dropping into local cafes for banana splits and double cokes, poured in to see film luminaries "in the flesh."

Everyone's noses were pressed against window panes lest they miss a chance to see Power, Fonda, or other members of the cast. Jim Denton was eating dinner with Donald Meek when he overheard a lady sigh with ecstatic relief "Oh, I've seen Donald Meek—now I can go home happy!"

Mary Clarke, young daughter of an Arkansas attorney, came to Noel with her mother. Power saw her and asked her if she would dance with him the next night. Much to her disappontment, she had to go home.

The highways were lined with cars and by late afternoon traffic was stalled for over a mile. In spite of the huge crowd, law-enforcement officials were able to keep some semblance of order. More than 18,000 cars were said to have been counted crossing the river bridge into Noel.

The Missouri highway patrolmen were the heroes of Johnnie Russell, who enacted the role of Jesse James, Jr. Russell became a favorite with the officers soon after his arrival in the Ozarks, and the patrolmen obtained permission from King and Russell's mother to take him on one of the inspection tours through the area. Russell returned home full of enthusiasm. "They've got machine guns, shotguns, pistols, and everything in their automobiles," he told his mother. "I'll bet they could give even Jesse James a tough battle."

Residents of Noel never dreamed that thousands of visitors would crowd into the town. As a result those who owned front and back yards were quick to realize an opportunity for extra profits. Cars had to be parked so they rented out what available space they had, charging a quarter per vehicle.

The only serious incident that occurred was the death of a little five-year-old girl. Her father, mother, brother, and sister had driven to Noel to catch a glimpse of the actors who arrived that morning. Her father said he had just parked his car when the little girl alighted, ran around the rear of the vehicle and into the path of an oncoming car. Her only desire had been to see a movie star.

That evening, at Shadow Lake, the stars and others of the troupe mingled with the natives and had a grand time. Miss Kelly was kept busy accepting invitations to dance and told reporters "that she was having a wonderful time and thought the people she had met were wonderful, too."

"Randy Scott is a very good dancer and has been teaching me a lot of new steps," she confided. "I guess I've danced more since I've been in the Ozarks than I have for ages, and I'm having such fun."

Power, Fonda, and Scott danced with local belles. "I've never been in a given area so crowded with good-looking girls in my life," remarked Power. "It's true we have beautiful girls in Hollywood, but they are brought there from every place in the world. In the Ozarks, they just come by it naturally. Beauty there is pretty unanimous." There were plenty of autograph seekers, and the stars thought it was fun writing in their books, on scraps of paper, hats, pocketbooks or anything else that was handy because they were so appreciative. Donlevy, Fonda, and Hull mixed a little fun with their autographing. Sometimes they would sign just any name that popped into their heads such as Lionel Barrymore, or Booker T. Washington. This made no difference to the autograph seeker.

Hull received the strangest request of any from a couple of

feminine fans. "Would you do something for us, Mr. Hull?" they asked. He asked them what they wanted. "Would you please just once say 'b'God and b'Jesus' like you did in *Tobacco Road*?"

Three records of *Alexander's Ragtime Band,* which had recently starred Power, were worn out as a tribute to him. After that he seldom turned on his radio, possibly fearing he would hear the song. The evening was cut short when director King informed those present that they had to be on location the next day at 5 a.m. He emphasized that he had a daily schedule to maintain, and delay would mean a loss of money, and at a cost of operation at $22,000 per day, time *was* money.

IV

THE MAKING OF JESSE JAMES

Occasionally a woman in the dense, shuffling crowd fainted from the heat, weariness, or the pressure of the elbows pushing against her ribs. When that happened, production stopped while the woman was revived.

On the first day of shooting, Tyrone Power and Henry Fonda were driven to a small cabin on the northern edge of Pineville, which had been constructed by the method known as "chink and daub." King was taken with the rustic structure, and used it as a background for the opening of the picture. The scene depicted Barshee, bullying representative of the St. Louis Midland, seated in his buggy with several of his men behind him, harassing a worried little farmer, who kept glancing unhappily at his frightened wife.

"Now listen, friend," said Barshee. "The railroad's going to come right smack through this land of yours and there ain't a thing in the world you can do to stop it."

"But Mister," said the farmer. "One dollar an acre! I paid fifteen dollars an acre for it—and there's my home—and my barn—and my crop!"

"Take it or leave it, friend, take it or leave it," said Barshee, "if you won't sell, all we got to do is call in the government. They'll confiscate your land and then you'll get NOTHING!"

"Mister," said the farmer. "I reckon...if that's the way they gonna git it."

"Now you're talking sense!" said Barshee. Taking the deed out of his vest pocket, he asked the farmer, "Can you write?" "No," was his reply. "Just put a cross here," smiled Barshee.

Later that day, Barshee applied the pressure to an elderly woman. Beside her stood her son. He gave her the same speech as the farmer and almost convinced her to sign. But her son wanted her to wait until they saw the Judge. "It won't do any good," explained Barshee. "But whatever you say, ma'am!" Turning to the boy he remarked, "All right son, no hard feelings."

He offered his hand and the boy, surprised, took it. Barshee jerked him forward, and swung with his left, knocking the boy down. As the boy started to rise angrily, Barshee kicked him. Barshee's escort moved nearer while the mother rose and pulled at Barshee. She pleaded for her boy's safety and ended up signing the deed.

King was faced with a difficult problem of eliminating the noise of automobile motors, as most of the scenes were near highways. The

Missouri Highway Patrol sent in all of its available officers to block off the roads, however, a dozen or more scenes were ruined until the deputy sheriff delivered the ultimatum that "the first one who lets out a peep while the next scene is bein' taken will be fined five dollars."

Occasionally a woman in the dense, shuffling crowd fainted from the heat, weariness, or the pressure of the elbows pushing against her ribs. When that happened, production stopped while the woman was revived. There were some problems that King and the deputy sheriff had not figured on. A dramatic scene was spoiled by a dog barking up a tree and a rooster crowing loudly during each "take." Exasperated, King finally shouted "QUIET" and the crowing stopped abruptly.

King had to order many retakes of scenes. With the temperature at a steady 100 degrees or better, the entire cast had been getting redder and redder in the face with each exposure to the sun. To the four makeup experts on the ground the process had been so gradual they failed to notice it. But when the studio makeup man saw the clips he immediately detected the difference. The faces showed too much red for technicolor filming.

To meet the situation, the studio was connected by teletype with Pineville. After viewing the clips the studio had been able to consult with the makeup men and told them how to correct the daily variations in the facial appearance of the players.

In Noel, where the film stars were virtually mobbed on arrival, townspeople were gradually getting back to normal, although Power and Fonda still had to be careful about appearing too frequently in public. At first, they were Mr. Power and Mr. Fonda, but after they had been in town for two or three days the townfolk began to regard them as old friends. At their insistence they were soon greeted with "Hello, Ty," and "Howdy, Hank."

When they began filming at the Crowder farm, King welcomed visitors, but was forced to have the roadway leading to the home blocked off, in order that the delicate sound instruments might not pick up the roar of automobile motors. Ingenious motorists discovered another road, but it was across the river from the Crowder farm. The natives, hearing their plight, paddled boats to the scene and ferried the visitors across the river for a fee of twenty-five cents—after which there was another charge of twenty-five cents for standing on the other side of the river to watch the proceedings.

Several young girls slipped onto the lawn and asked a couple of bit players for their autographs. They had to be escorted off the lot. "We tried to outsmart the crowd," said Power, "by starting work at daylight, but we found our audience waiting for us. In fact, one farmer complained about our late start. He had milked five cows, fed his pigs, driven into town, and arrived an hour too early!"

Filming commenced showing Jesse cutting firewood when Barshee and his men rode up. Barshee asked him if he owned this farm and Jesse responded that his mother did.

Mrs. Samuel, seated in a chair under an old tree, was shelling butter beans in her lap. Barshee went through his usual routine, but Mrs. Samuel was not interested. Becoming impatient, he told her that "either you'll take what I'm offering everybody else or you'll get nothing...and we'll get the land just the same!"

Mrs. Samuel was still insistent on not signing the deed. Barshee said he did not want any trouble with her. Frank told him, "Didn't you hear her say no?"

Lunging to his feet, Frank moved toward his mother. Barshee chuckled, and said, "Well, whatever you folks say!"

Barshee offered his hand and Frank took it. Once more Barshee gripped and pulled, but Frank swung faster, and Barshee went down.

"Kinda tricky, ain't you!" said Frank.

"Yea?" said Barshee. Turning to his men he ordered them to "take him!"

Jesse fired a warning shot and inquired whether or not they were all going to jump on Frank. He asked Frank if he wanted to fight him.

"If you'll keep them fellows from running up my back," said Frank.

Barshee charged him like a bull, and a fight followed. They clawed, gouged, rolled the ground, and swung from their heels, with no holds barred.

Everyone was quiet. Without a word, Donlevy and Fonda went into a clinch. Suddenly a raucous din of guinea-fowl chatter floated in, ruining the sound effects. "What's that?" asked King. Mrs. Crowder explained that those were her prized guineas. Robert Webb put in a session of haggling with her, then bought them from her for thirty-five cents apiece. Helped by a sweating, swearing crew of carpenters, electricians and handymen, he rounded up the fowls and sold them to a local butcher.

When King began his next day's work, more guinea hens squawked and fussed on the farm. Webb thought he had deguineaed. He bought these guineas too. For several days he bought guinea hens every day and sold them to the butcher. It seemed to Webb that these guinea hens must have guinea-pig blood. Finally he discovered that he had been buying and selling the same guineas over and over. The butcher had been bringing them back to Mrs. Crowder's farm every morning at daybreak. It was merely a case of native shrewdness outsmarting a man from a big city who carried a thick roll of bills in his pocket. After all, a well-known yardstick applied to any business deal concerns the motto "let the purchaser beware," and this taught Webb to protect himself in such dealings.

"We stopped that guinea buying in a hurry," Webb said. "We ate them whether in the mood or not."

Nancy Kelly mentioned her distaste of the guinea menu and wished she had a steak for dinner. A proprietor of a Noel meat market overheard the remark, and that afternoon sent her a steak so huge that Miss Kelly gave a dinner party for several members of the cast.

A sizable number of sight-seers from Neosho had gone to Noel for a glimpse of Power. Those who stayed at home got to see him, and some even got his autograph. Power had made a trip to Neosho, apparently to purchase a few sport shirts and to get a soft drink at a drug store.

Unrecognized, Power walked into a men's store and was busily engaged in selecting shirts when a salesman from Cincinnati "broke the news" that "Jesse" was in town. In a few minutes, the store began to fill with the curious and Power began to edge out. The clerk who sold the shirts, proudly exhibited the actor's autograph. Power then went to a nearby drugstore for refreshments, but left by a back door when a crowd appeared at the front.

Brian Donlevy upset the script and turned the villain into a hero. Donlevy was making a triumphant entry into the Missouri town of Sedalia in a buggy pulled by a spirited horse. Preceding him was the town band and a group of small boys, and following him were several hundred bit players garbed as townspeople.

At least 1,000 natives and visitors had gathered around the square to watch the filming when suddenly, Donlevy's horse bolted, knocked down a trumpet player in the band, and headed directly for the side-lines of extras too frightened to move. He pulled back on the reins quickly enough to halt the horse's mad rush until members of the film company could grab the animal, thereby averting an accident which might have resulted in serious injury to Donlevy as well as to many of the bystanders.

Crag O'Lea cave, just north of Pineville, formed the setting for the most intimate scenes. There Jesse and Frank James went into hiding following the wounding of Barshee. Meanwhile, Barshee had seen the sheriff and obtained a warrant for the James boys' arrest. Barshee arrived at the James farm to serve the warrant himself. Afraid to go inside, he threatened to "blow them out" if they didn't surrender, but only Mrs. Samuel was inside.

Mrs. Samuel, hearing Barshee's warning, attempted to get out of bed to let him come in. Major Cobb told Barshee that "she's bad sick and in bed, and her heart won't stand you mules tromping through the house."

Barshee still believed it was all a trick. "Well I got a way to find out," he told the Major, as he pulled a hand grenade from his saddle-bag.

He issued the ultimatum that "James, if you ain't outa there in one minute, with your hands up, I'm gonna blow you out!"

Stumbling toward the front door, holding to chairs, Mrs. Samuel attempted to tell them that her sons had left. But with a crash and darkness, the table against which she had lurched fell over, the lamp breaking on the floor.

"What did I tell you!" yelled Barshee as he drew back his arm.

The hand grenade splintered through a front window of the house as the farmers closed recklessly on the posse and grappled for the riders, horses' heads, heedless of the pistol blows and threats. But almost at the same instant, there was a scream of terror from the house, and then a deafening explosion. Windows shattered, the whole house buckled, a blinding smoke screened the scene.

A few minutes later, in the background, farmers were fighting the flames that swept the wrecked house. In the foreground Mrs. Samuel, eyes closed, blood on her face, lay still on blankets spread on the ground, her head pillowed on other blankets. Beside her kneeled the Major. Sullen and angry Barshee looked down at her. A farmer's wife was cleaning Mrs. Samuel's face.

Miss Darwell spent hours lying on a blanket in the lawn of the Crowder farm pretending to be dead. She was given the appearance of death after makeup men had dabbed artificial blood at the corners of her mouth as though she were bleeding. Expert technicians went about the business of burning the home, a difficult job to do without harming the structure. Long smoke fuses which, when ignitied, sent smoke billowing from the windows, were placed back of each window. Also, inside the windows were placed metal troughs in which chemical flames were created.

While the crowds were large each day at Noel, and at the scene of operations, Labor Day was another record breaker in the number of people who visited the vicinity. Though no definite check was made, it was estimated that the crowd was nearly 50,000.

There was plenty of action on the set for the visitors when scenes depicting an attempt to burn the home of the James brothers gave native extras a chance to play their parts as volunteer firemen. It was estimated approximately 150 residents of the community were used in the various scenes.

The crowd which eventually gathered around the home had the unique experience of seeing King film the final scene of the picture. That scene depicted Henry Hull as Major Cobb, newspaper editor friend of the James brothers, delivering the eulogy at Jesse James' grave while sorrowing friends and relatives hovered nearby.

"Jesse was an outlaw, a bandit, a criminal," said the Major. "But we aren't ashamed of him. Maybe it's because we understand a little that he wasn't to blame for what his times made him. All I know is, he was one of the doggonedest, dadblamedest buckaroos that ever rode across the United States of America."

One man came up to Henry King and said he was Jesse James. "As a matter of fact," said King, "he bore a striking resemblance to the famous outlaw. And he was familiar with every detail of James' life. He said that Bob Ford hadn't killed him." It was discovered later that he was just a harmless old fellow who lived near Pineville. "But he sure scared me for a minute," said King. "It would be embarrassing to no end to find after making *Jesse James* that the outlaw himself was sitting in the balcony watching it!"

Visibly fatigued after a week on location under a hot sun, the actors and other members of the company were looking forward to a brief respite from the grind. Several amusing incidents occurred in which the stars had figured. A young woman obtained special permission to take a snapshot of Power, and then became so excited she turned the camera around and snapped a picture of herself. Power heard about the incident by accident, and promptly had a large autographed photograph of himself sent to the young woman.

Shortly thereafter, a young lady walked up to Power and told him a friend had made her a wager she would be unable to shake hands with the young star. Power not only shook hands, but chatted with the young lady several minutes. Meanwhile, the woman's husband had been busy recording the meeting with the motion picture camera. "You won't have any trouble proving you won that bet now, honey," he told his wife.

Fonda had been particularly impressed with the acting ability of the natives employed as extras in the various scenes. "I saw a young mother with a baby on the set the other day whose naturalness of actions was to me real art," he told his friends. "I can see that we actors are going to have to work hard during this picture so that it won't appear that we are just acting."

Francis Adams, Power's lifelong friend and business manager, spent a weekend in Noel, but decided he preferred the comparative peace and quiet of Hollywood.

"I never saw anything like the crowds here," Adams told Power. "Never before have I seen the people of any section of the country go so completely mad about the filming of a picture."

Power's business manager's troubles began shortly after he arrived in the hill country, when someone mistook him for Lionel Barrymore. The rumor spread like wildfire, and soon Adams was surrounded by so many autograph seekers he was at his wits end. He finally solved the problem by bidding Power a hasty goodbye and driving to Tulsa to catch a plane for the west coast.

Meanwhile, the stars had been taking advantage of their leisure moments to go swimming and fishing. They had discarded their expensive rods and reels since learning the natives had better luck with soft-shell crawfish bait and cane poles. The natives had been doing a big business procuring the crawfish for the stars at the standard rate of twenty-five cents a dozen.

On his first day out, Fonda, an avid deep-sea fisherman, caught a seven and one-half pound catfish. Scott and Chaney told reporters, "we caught 200 pounds but only brought back a few ounces." But Scott's story was different. "I reeled in the line," he said, "and out of the water came, of all things, a new fountain pen in good working order." Instead of stopping right there, Scott carried the tale further by claiming that a huge fish came to the bank of the stream and said, "Autograph, please."

Not to be outdone, Carradine purchased a rod and reel and numerous lures and started out on an expedition on his own. When he returned he reported dejectedly he did not even get a nibble.

Deciding that perhaps the tackle was at fault, Carradine the following day purchased a new outfit and new lures. Again he failed to get a bite, and he finally gave up in frustration.

"I guess someone must have told the fish here I'm the villain in the picture," he sighed.

"No, it isn't that," remarked Fonda. "these h'yar fish are not u'd to sophisticated worms."

Nancy Kelly as Zee

Nancy Kelly, Tyrone Power

Henry Hull, Nancy Kelly

Randolph Scott as Marshal Will Wright

Nancy Kelly, Randolph Scott, Johnnie Russell

Randolph Scott, unidentified extra

Nancy Kelly, Randolph Scott

Henry Hull

Henry Hull, two unidentified extras

Tyrone Power, Henry Fonda, Henry Hull

Henry Hull, Johnnie Russell, George Chandler

Brian Donlevy as Barshee

Brian Donlevy

Brian Donlevy

Jane Darwell

Henry Fonda, Jane Darwell, Tyrone Power

The cast and crew take a break, waiting for a "take" in front of the marshal's office and the Liberty *Weekly Gazette.* The view is on the Pineville square, on the south side, looking west from the southeast corner.

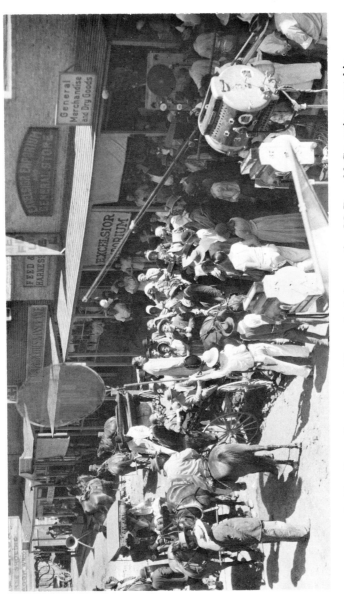

Dabbs Greer (in center with mustache), a native McDonald Countian, got his start in the movie. He now appears in the "*Little House on the Prairie*" television series. The scene is on the east side of the Pineville square.

Chink and daub cabin used in the film

Salt-Peter Cave, one mile east of Pineville on Big Sugar Creek, served as Jesse's hideout. It was here that Zee came to tell the brothers of their mother's death.

The Drumm building was the pay office. Extras and drivers received two dollars and a half a day, horses a dollar. Use of a vehicle added another fifty cents.

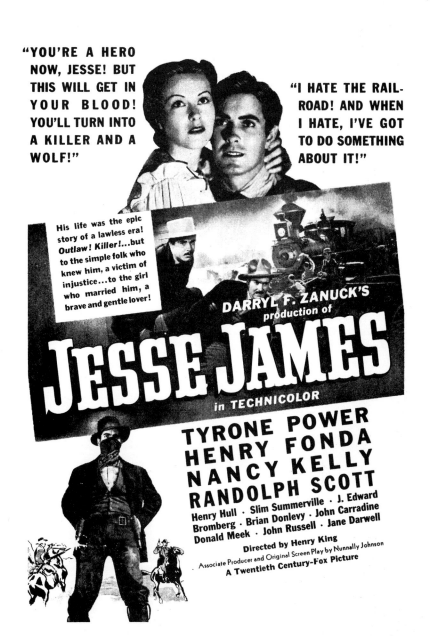

"YOU'RE A HERO NOW, JESSE! BUT THIS WILL GET IN YOUR BLOOD! YOU'LL TURN INTO A KILLER AND A WOLF!"

"I HATE THE RAILROAD! AND WHEN I HATE, I'VE GOT TO DO SOMETHING ABOUT IT!"

His life was the epic story of a lawless era! *Outlaw! Killer!*...but to the simple folk who knew him, a victim of injustice...to the girl who married him, a brave and gentle lover!

DARRYL F. ZANUCK'S
production of

JESSE JAMES

in TECHNICOLOR

TYRONE POWER
HENRY FONDA
NANCY KELLY
RANDOLPH SCOTT

Henry Hull · Slim Summerville · J. Edward Bromberg · Brian Donlevy · John Carradine Donald Meek · John Russell · Jane Darwell

Directed by Henry King
Associate Producer and Original Screen Play by Nunnally Johnson
A Twentieth Century-Fox Picture

The Studio widely publicized the movie, depicting Jesse as a misunderstood man.

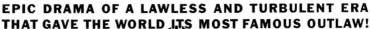

The Studio widely publicized the movie, depicting Jesse as a hero.

V

JESSE JAMES, THE LEGEND

Jesse decided that his mother's death must be avenged. He left Zee with Frank, and told her that "It might be a long time before I'll see you again."

Otto Brower was sent by the studio to supervise the filming of background scenes. After conferring with King, Brower and his staff made their way deep into the hill country to film a series of scenic shots. Upon his return, Brower noticed he was being bothered by an itching sensation on his right arm, and he sought out the company physician. "Don't be alarmed, Otto, it's nothing serious," the doctor assured him, "but you'll probably be itching for some time. You're suffering from poison ivy."

During the filming of a background scene near Pineville a goat wandered onto the set. "Get that goat out of the way," ordered Brower.

Brower's assistants rushed to do his bidding, but retreated in disorder when the goat lowered its head and rushed toward them. Brower, a moment later, also was forced to retreat when the animal rushed toward the camera.

One of the crew members, an expert with a lariat, finally solved the problem by neatly lassoing the goat. It remained tied to a tree during the film expressing its disgust in no uncertain terms with frequent "baas."

Crag O'Lea cave was the setting for the scene where Zee carried the news to Jesse and Frank that their mother was dead. Brower was required to use a dapple horse, but the animal became so skittish the director's assistants were unable to hold the horse still.

Finally, in desperation, Brower obtained a white horse whose gentle nature was well known. One of his assistants transformed the animal into a dapple horse with the aid of a brush and Miss Kelly began to practice riding side saddle on it.

While practicing her stirrup broke, and she fell from the horse against a barbed-wire fence. The jagged wire ripped through the heavy dress and two petticoats, but she escaped with minor scratches, and was able to return to the set after being given treatment. Fortunately, the wardrobe department had brought along an extra duplicate of the dress Miss Kelly was required to wear in the scene, and no time was lost.

Jesse decided that his mother's death must be avenged. He left Zee with Frank, and told her that "It might be a long time before I'll see you again." "I...I can wait," responded Zee.

Jesse rode into Liberty where he headed for the Dixie Belle Saloon. Inside Jesse stopped and looked around. At the rear of the room, Barshee was laughing and talking with two of his men, until the silence called his attention to something unusual. He then saw Jesse.

Jesse told Barshee to "keep your hands in sight." Slowly, Barshee put his glass down. He faced death and knew it.

"Count three and duck," said Jesse to the bartender.

Barshee began to plead with Jesse and told him "It was an accident! I swear it was!" But Jesse paid no attention other than tell the bartender to count.

Unnoticed, Lynch, Barshee's lieutenant drew his pistol and fired. But there were two shots, and Lynch, toppled forward as Jesse's gun swung back on Barshee just as the latter drew, but not fast enough. Barshee was dead.

Following the shooting, it was Power's cue to back out of the saloon. At least one scene was ruined when bystanders, seeing him, involuntarily shouted, "There he is!"

Later that day Power went on a short trip to Tulsa, Oklahoma, without any money and had to make a telephone call back to Noel. "I had a nickel to get the operator with in a pay booth," said Power, "but when I wanted to put through a collect call the operator asked, 'Who's calling?' "

"Tyrone Power," he replied.

"Quit your fooling," she said. "I'm a busy person. Give me your name and I'll put the call through."

Power tried to explain, but none of the operators would give him a chance. They were enjoying the conversation when a voice said, "It is Tyrone Power. I recognize his voice. I'd know it anywhere."

The voice insisted and put the call through for Power. He learned her name and invited her to dinner. They spent a grand evening, dining and dancing at Shadow Lake resort.

The next day's filming resumed with Jesse and Frank becoming hunted fugitives. In one of the scenes, Jesse and Frank dealt with a posse from which they fled by scattering paper money along the trail. The members of the posse leaped from their horses to pick up the bills, enabling the outlaws to escape.

In order to provide an added incentive for members of the posse, Brower instructed an assistant to mark certain bills. He told them each marked bill would be worth one dollar in cash.

Considerable pains had been taken to place the posse on a wooded hill. Finally, the posse came tearing down the hill just as an old hound dog flushed out a rabbit a short distance from the camera. Hound and rabbit raced into the group of horsemen. The frightened horses plunged and reared, and they had to start all over again.

When filming resumed there was a mad scramble for the money. Brower was elated. Then he found out that all the other extras, who had gathered along the sidelines, had joined in thereby ruining the scene. He solved the problem by prohibiting everyone except those necessary for the scene from the set. "Gosh, I don't blame them," he later commented, "I almost jumped in there myself!"

Brower had on occasion, employed 100 or more extras as members of a cavalry unit. They appeared at the location site, resplendent in blue uniforms, with shining sabers hanging from their belts. It was at that particular moment that the camera crew discovered their vision would be partly obscured by dense underbrush.

"I guess there's nothing else to do but have you generals come down off your high horses and go to work," said Brower. Shortly thereafter, visitors were treated to the unusual spectacle of an entire cavalry unit cutting underbrush with their sabers.

Brower revealed that he had requested one of his assistants to obtain a trotting horse so he might judge the correct speed for a chase sequence. "They brought thirty horses to me, and every one of them turned out to be a pacer," he explained, "so that's how I happened to be out there on the road playing the role of a trotting horse."

The posse sent out to capture Jesse was pressed into service on an actual man hunt several days later when assistant director Hal Herman was reported missing. Herman had ridden with another crew member from Pineville to Noel where he was staying. He had left orders for an assistant to drive his own automobile to Noel later.

Through error the assistant neglected to deliver the car, and when a night watchman found Herman's automobile, the word went out that he was missing. The posse finally found Herman sleeping peacefully in his bed at Noel.

King spent a strenuous afternoon staging a train robbery on a section of railroad track which ran alongside a huge bluff between Noel and Lanagan. The location was some distance from the road, but several hundred sight-seers tramped their way through the brush for four miles, some of them fording Indian creek to get a better view. One farmer opened a road through the woods by chopping out the undergrowth; he then charged twenty-five cents to drive down to the edge of the cliff.

A young girl asked Power if she could get on the train. "You see," she said, "I've never been on a train in my life before, and this is the first chance I have ever had." Her charm was so compelling that Power took her to King. "Why bless your soul," he exclaimed, "I should say you can get on that train." King not only put her on the train, but placed her in a shot involving Randolph Scott and Donald Meek.

Lon Chaney, Jr., while playing a member of the James gang, slipped and sustained a badly sprained ankle. During the filming of the train robbery, the cinch strap on his horse broke, throwing him from the horse and causing an injury to his knee. "I guess I'll probably break my leg next," commented Chaney.

At dusk, with its windows lighted and its whistle sounding, the train puffed its way down the tracks. Galloping alongside the train, Jesse leaped aboard the rear platform. He peered through the rear door window at the passengers, and then began to climb to the roof, to make his way forward to the engine.

Power was silhouetted against the deepening blue of the sky, while the car windows below him glowed with orange lamplight. This scene provided a striking and economical contrast between the cold, dangerous world of the outlaw and the warm, comfortable world of the law-abiding passengers.

"Slack up at this next curve," said Jesse to the engineer, "and stop her just this side of that clump of trees around the bend."

As the train slowed, the band, led by Frank, broke from the clump of trees and galloped down on the train. Frank then directed a brakeman to uncouple the engine from the rest of the train.

The passengers were buzzing with fear and excitement when Bob Ford entered. "If you don't know what this is folks, it's a holdup," he said, "and don't forget to sue the railroad for whatever you give us because it's responsible."

King had been able to maintain his original schedule, despite the fact that insects, overcast skies, and rain threatened to delay the scenes for several days. During those days, cover or interior shots were filmed.

One of these was the scene depicting the meeting of Jesse and his sweetheart, Zee, in the back room of the Liberty *Weekly Gazette*, following the train robbery. Major Cobb and Zee were staring at a rear window, where Jesse's face appeared and smirked at them. Much amused by his own humor, Jesse started to edge his way in, clowning, but Zee jerked him into the room and quickly shut the door.

Greetings were exchanged and Jesse learned that the marshal had thirty men out after him. Shortly thereafter Will Wright, the U. S. marshal, paid an unexpected visit to Zee, and came face to face with Jesse, who was introduced as Mister Howard. Jesse became uneasy. Wright told him, in no certain terms, that if Jesse and he ever met, "it's just going to be me or him."

Wright, whose secret love for Zee made him lenient toward Jesse, was persuaded, by railroad president McCoy, to convince Jesse to surrender. Wright extracted a written promise from him, which promised nominal prosecution for the desperado. Zee took it to Jesse. Surprised at her manner he read it, and looked at her in bewilderment. At first he thought it was a trick, but he finally decided to turn himself in. He asked Zee if she would marry him now. Her reply was yes.

Mill Creek Baptist Church, built years ago in a secluded dell near the town of Noel, formed the setting for the marriage of Zee and Jesse. It was Sunday noon. Up the wooded road came a procession led by Frank. Following him came a buggy bearing Jesse and Zee. Accompanying the bridal party were the other bandits.

Farmers had a good laugh when two cows strayed onto the set

71

while King was filming the wedding scene. "Somebody get those cows out of the way," shouted King. The assistant director rushed to do his bidding. "Come bossies—nice bossies, get off the set," he pleaded, beckoning to them with his hands. The animals continued to chew their cuds placidly, until several of the farmers drove the cows back into the woods.

Jesse and Zee started into the church as the preacher was delivering his sermon. He stopped as the congregation stared at the entrance of the bridal party. As Jesse and Zee looked uncomfortably around the preacher said, "welcome, brothers and sisters."

"Could we get hitched?" asked Jesse. The preacher consented. He asked their names. The effect on the congregation was electric. At the same time the groomsmen, deployed strategically about the church. "All right, we're gathered here to join Zerelda Mimms and Jesse Woodson James in the bonds of holy matrimony," said the preacher.

Jesse met Will the next day and turned over his guns to him. They proceeded into town to the courthouse. Jesse was told by the judge that "I'm aiming to go as light as the law allows, Jesse, and when you come out, the slate'll be clean. The past'll all be forgot."

Zee and Jesse said good-bye for a couple of hours, before King got the take he wanted. Power enfolded Miss Kelly and her flounces in a close embrace and rubbed the right side of his face against hers. "My darling! My wife!" he murmured.

"My husband!" whispered Miss Kelly. "I'm proud of you, Jesse, proud of you!" they kissed, and kissed again, and broke apart. Power marched back to the cell.

Walking out of the cell, which had no side walls, he joined Miss Kelly, who was rubbing her chin. "You're ruining my face!" she said. "You and your whiskers! Two more kisses and there won't be a shred of skin left." Power grinned unsympathetically, "you're just out of practice, Nancy. Do you know how tough I am with women? Why, one time I met my mother on the train and broke two of her ribs hugging her. We didn't find it out for a couple of days, but I told her she'd have to get used to that kind of treatment to be my gal."

When filming resumed, Jesse looked around the cell. There was a small, barred window at one end. As he sat down, he heard the sound of squeaking shoes along the stone corridor. The footsteps stopped.

McCoy introduced himself and informed Jesse that "I just want to welcome you, and tell you how glad I am to see you here...in jail." Jesse realized that he had been duped.

Will had been out of town, and as he rode into town, he was puzzled by the sight of the military. He elbowed his way through the crowd into the courthouse. He questioned McCoy and was told that the district of Liberty had been placed under martial law.

McCoy expressed grave concern over Will's attitude and advised him to confine himself to the duties of his office. "Suppose Jesse don't WANT to be hanged!" said Will.

They all stared at him as he turned and walked out. Then they laughed, but it died suddenly when Pinkie, the James' Negro servant, delivered a note to McCoy which read, "Mr. McCoy, if Jesse ain't out of jail by midnight I'm a-coming in and git him. Frank James."

He read it aloud and they all laughed at the idea. He crumpled the note and tossed it. The jailor, seated, picked up the note and then, with a deep sigh, covered his eyes with one hand and moaned. "I've known Frank James for a long time, and if he says he aims to DO something he's liable to come pretty near DOING it!" he said. "You're crazy," said McCoy.

But the jailor shook his head as he looked up at the clock. McCoy was about to turn back to some papers when he cast a quick, worried glance at the clock. It said 11:45. The door then opened and Wright entered.

McCoy and Wright discussed the note, and it was decided to swear in additional deputies. They went to the Dixie Belle Saloon. Twenty or thirty volunteers clustered around Wright who with the unsolicited help of McCoy, picked the deputies.

Wright and McCoy returned to the courthouse. McCoy was chewing on a cigar and staring at the clock. As the minute hand hit twelve, the jailor's chair collasped with a crash.

"You...you...you," said McCoy.

"I couldn't help it. I'm just nervous, that's all. Frank said he was gonna give you to twelve to let Jesse out, and if he wasn't out by then..." said the jailor.

Frank was captured and wounded trying to elude a couple of deputies. As he was brought inside the courthouse, McCoy could scarcely conceal his relief and satisfaction. Will greeted Frank and told him that "all the honors belonged to Mr. McCoy."

Will looked at him, sighed, shrugged, and moved toward the door. "Goodnight, everybody," said Will. There was no response except "Goodnight, marshal," from Frank.

McCoy endeavored to control his temper while Frank rhythmically chewed his tobacco and watched him without expression. Frank told him that "You ought not to do this after we trusted you. You ought to keep your word." "The way you're going to keep yours," jeered McCoy. "Sir," responded a puzzled Frank. "You said you were going to take Jesse out of here!" said McCoy.

"I am," said Frank. He then instructed one of his men to lock the door.

Those in the room were told to "lay down or be shot down," and they all dropped to the floor. Jesse was released and the two brothers exchanged greetings. As they moved toward the inner office, they found McCoy and the others, lying spread-eagled on the floor.

McCoy's eyes widened with terror as Jesse knelt beside him. Jesse pulled the note which promised him nominal prosecution if he surrendered in good faith, and held it in front of McCoy's face.

"Don't! Don't kill me!" whispered McCoy.

"I ain't, not with a gun! Brother, I'm going to WORRY you to death," said Jesse.

With a quick sharp gesture he crammed the note into McCoy's mouth, forcing it all in, and then held his palm clamped over the mouth.

"Now chew! See how it tastes! And swallow!" said Jesse.

As McCoy chewed, his eyes were bulging. "Give him some water when we leave, to wash it down," said Jesse. The brothers then dashed from the town on horseback, firing their pistols as they fled.

As Fonda departed, his .45 caliber revolver, loaded with blank shells, was discharged by accident and the cartridge bruised the calf of his leg. The actor was taken to the hospital for a tetanus shot.

Jesse and Zee went into hiding, but after their baby was born, Zee went back to Liberty with the Major. Jesse had decided to resume his outlaw career.

The take for this scene was ruined when a woman dashed between the camera and complained to Webb that the crowds had drunk her well dry. Sighing, but unstumped, Webb ordered a 1,500 gallon tank rolled to the river's edge, had it filled and replenished the well.

J. Edward Bromberg was chosen to play the role of George Runyan, detective assigned to bring the outlaw reign of the James brothers to an end. "You'll notice in the *Jesse James* script that Runyan engages in his villainous practices, but is perpetually smiling or beaming throughout the picture," he said. "That's a new angle for a villain's role," Bromberg continued, "and I am greatly interested in seeing what I can do with the difficult characterization."

One morning shortly after daylight, Bromberg, stood shivering on one of the sets while workmen were assembling equipment. "This," he said, "is one of those sort of mornings when the stars fight with their stand-ins for the privilege of standing in front of the klieg lights."

Time had passed and a score or more of well-dressed men, bankers, were seated at random about the office of the Governor of Missouri listening intently to the words of George Runyan, chief of the Runyan Detective Agency. "The obvious solution of course," stated Runyan, "is to destroy this band by destroying its leader, Jesse James. Fortunately for us, the band contains a traitor."

The governor was persuaded to promise amnesty, and a clean pardon, in addition to the reward, to any member of the James gang who would kill Jesse. Runyan left for Liberty to locate Bob Ford. Unable to find him he left his card and the paper telling about the pardon with Mrs. Ford.

Jesse was interested in robbing the First National Bank at Northfield, Minnesota, but there was no response from his gang. He became upset when one of his gang spoke up saying, "we don't exactly know if we like this idea or not." After some discussion it was decided that Northfield was all right to hit.

Bob Ford notified Runyan of the plan and told him not to shoot him as he would be riding a gray horse. Runyan proceeded to Northfield where he informed the bank president that the James' gang were on their way. "Great thundering hallelujah! That's ruin! They'll take everything! I've got $50,000," replied the president. "Easy! Easy! There's not danger, don't you see? I'm here!" said Runyan.

Jesse and two of his gang rode up the street. They wore long white coats, which gave them an air of respectability and also concealed their arms. They attracted no attention; but when they turned off the side street and into the main street, four men emerged from a house and began to stretch a barricade of wagons across the street.

Jesse and his men reined up at a hitching rack in front of a saloon. They were about to enter the saloon when Jesse's attention was drawn to a display of rifles and shotguns in a hardware store window that was situated between the saloon on one side and the bank on the other. In front of the window, Jesse pointed to the gun he wished he could own. As he continued to look, Ford, and two others walked up from the opposite direction. At the right of the bank, Ford dismounted from his horse and looked uneasy, his eyes darted around for signs of the trap.

Ambling up the street, Frank's face broke into a broad smile as he pulled up in front of the hardware store.

"Why, cousin Bushrod!" said Frank.

"Well, if it ain't cousin Beauregard!" said Jesse.

"Howdy, cousin! How are you?" said Frank.

"Beauregard, I ain't seen you in a coon's age!" said Jesse.

"Come on in the bank with me, I got to git some money changed! How's Aunt Mary Lou? How's the twins?" asked Frank.

As they entered, one of the gang walked over and closed the bank door after them. At this point the town bell began to toll in the church steeple in the background, and men stepped indoors, while women pulled their children along toward side streets and safety.

Frank and Jesse were at the teller's window. As the bell continued to toll, Jesse looked around convinced that something wrong was afoot.

Runyan was peering through a hole in the door of the president's office. Then he stepped back and lifted the rifle to level it through the hole. Frank stepped to the teller's counter and reached into his pocket. Laying a bill on the counter, Frank asked, "Can you change this for me, colonel?'' ''I'll have to go in the safe. If you'll just wait here,'' replied the teller. As he hurried toward the rear of the bank, Jesse looked around positive now that trouble was on its way.

As Runyan sighted his rifle through the slit in the door, there was a shot and Jesse went down. Instantly Frank fired at the office door. One of the gang ran to pick up Jesse, who was already staggering to his feet, his gun in his hand.

Covering their rear with shots at the windows and the doors, the four outlaws started for the street door. Both hands occupied, Frank kicked the door open.

The James gang was shot apart in the ill-fated robbery. Jesse and Frank escaped the massacre. Frank managed to aid his wounded brother in the getaway as Jesse was having trouble keeping on his horse. Frank, wounded also, but less seriously, slowed down. The posse came galloping in pursuit.

As Jesse and Frank approached a small hill, Jesse slipped from his horse to the ground. Frank sprung from the saddle and helped him to his feet. ''We got to keep goin', son! Now hold tight, Jesse because there ain't but one way outa here!'' Frank lashed the horse, which lunged up the little hill, reared at the tip, and dove smack into the water. Jesse was swept away and was thought to have drowned. Frank then dove his horse smack into the water.

Jesse's horse swam away as Frank's horse came snorting to the surface, followed by Frank, also snorting. Frank grabbed his horses tail, and looked around anxiously. ''Jesse!'' he called but never received an answer. On the cliff a mounted member of the posse took aim again. He fired, then yelled and waved as a signal to other members.

Frank's horse plunged out of the water up the bank, with him hanging to the horse's tail. Then he swung astride, looked again at the water for Jesse, and as another bullet sung past him, galloped away into some woods.

When the first unit of the *Jesse James* company returned to Hollywood, the second unit, directed by Otto Brower, was sent by

Henry King to film what later became the most controversial of all sequences, the escape of Jesse and Frank James from the Northfield bank raid by jumping off a cliff while on their horses.

Cliff Lyons, stuntman, performed the stunt in which he fell with a horse, one hundred feet from the edge of a cliff into water. He was reported to have received $750 for each jump, a considerable sum in those days, particularly since several takes were required.

The incident that arose stemmed from the fact that Brower had let an amateur cameraman photograph the whole scene. "Later this man went to New York and wanted to sell the film to the studio for $25,000," reminisced King, "and they asked, what film? The amateur remarked, 'If you don't give me the money I will take another recourse.' So he got the Humane Society, the press, and everybody together and ran it for them."

Sydney Coleman, president of the Society for the Prevention of Cruelty to Animals, in a letter to Will Hayes, president of the Motion Picture Producers and Distributors of America, protested against alleged acts of cruelty to animals in the filming of movies and asked that steps be taken to see that certain "atrocities" were not repeated.

Coleman cited Twentieth Century-Fox studio as having gone to "incredible lengths of inhuman cruelty to horses" in making *Jesse James* and added that the association would advise nearly 600 anti-cruelty societies in the United States to voice their disapproval to all film companies, to local theater managers, and to Will Hayes, against the practices of running horses off cliffs, and tripping them with wires.

The protest was based in part upon sworn affidavits of eyewitnesses, obtained by the managing director of the Humane Society of Missouri, from residents of Camden County, Missouri, where the film was taken, that the horse was blindfolded and led to a chute with a rocker attachment. The weight of the horse tipped the chute toward a greased slide, the witness charged, and the animal plunged off a one hundred foot cliff into space, landed upon its hindquarters and drowned apparently because it was unable to swim.

Coleman said its carcass was removed only because the movie company valued the saddle and bridle, and wanted back its property to place on another horse which was forced to go through the same procedure. He added that the second horse missed the greased saddle and struck a projecting rock, but was not killed.

"What had happened," said King, "was that the horse slipped on the slide, and when it reached bottom, hit some stones thinking it was solid ground. Unfortunately, it put its head down, breathed through the nostrils, which only took a few seconds before the animal died. The stuntman, who had been thrown from the horse, swam to shore uninjured."

Visibly shaken by his first experience, the stuntman climbed into the saddle on the second horse. This time, as the horse made the descent, the slide broke, which caused the stuntman to be thrown against the side of the cliff. The crew thought he had been killed or mangled for life, but to their astonishment, survived and actually completed the scene, after having suffered only minor cuts and bruises.

S. R. Kent, president of Twentieth Century-Fox, made public a letter to Coleman denying charges made by him of cruelty to horses in *Jesse James*. He admitted that there was an "injury" to one of the horses during the shooting of a scene on the top of a cliff in the Missouri Ozarks, but added that "the very fact that the scene was repeated without injury to either horse or rider was definite proof that it was purely accidental and not because we were compelling either horse or rider to take an unnecessary risk."

"The same rider rode all the horses that were used in the scene," the letter added, "and the original accident was caused by a premature fall of one of the horses. In our opinion, Twentieth Century-Fox is no more responsible for this accident than a polo player would be if he fell in a game of polo and one of his ponies was injured."

Kent further stated that representatives of Coleman's organization had for three years "watched us at our request whenever we were shooting a picture with animals and that never once has your organization questioned our purpose or motive." He even expressed surprise that, though the film was made months ago and a representative of the society was apparently "on the ground," no criticism or disapproval was received until after the picture had been released in New York. The scene was regarded by theater audiences as one of the spectacular highlights of the movie.

Painfully, Jesse made his way home to St. Joseph where Zee nursed him back to health and convinced him to go straight. The two decided it was time to start all over again. They planned to go to California with their son, until their dream was interrupted by the appearance of Bob and Charley Ford.

Bob and Charley tried to persuade Jesse to come with them and meet Frank. They had plans to rob another bank. Jesse listened with keen interest and almost decided to go, but his thinking was interrupted. The yammer of children's voices rose louder outside the window. Jesse James, Jr., was yelling "I want to come in."

"All right, come in, but stop that hollering!" said Jesse. but the yammering of the children became a frantic clamor. He excused himself, but stopped short of exiting, as he was asked if he was going to walk around outside with them guns? He unbuckled the belt and hung it on a chair. Charley, rose, his gun half out, when Bob grabbed his wrist in terror. Jesse, his back to them, had not noticed. He went outside and picked the child up and carried him upstairs.

In tears with fear and anxiety, Zee stood with hands damp and tight when Jesse entered. For a moment he looked with affection into the child's face and then kissed him. Then he told Zee to get him ready as "we're catching the afternoon train." Jesse had made a decision that was irrevocable. The Fords regarded him questioningly, but Jesse told them to tell Frank "he better pick up and come and join me while the joinin's good."

As the Fords left, Zee ran down the stairs, too happy for words, singing to the tune of *O Susannah*. "Oh, Mr. Howard! We have got to run! Cause we're going to California on the train this afternoon!"

"Yes, Mrs. Howard! And what can I do to help!" responded Jesse.

The Ford brothers stood on the porch just outside the door, and listened in sullen anger to the festivity inside. Charley decided to go ahead, stepped off the porch and peered cautiously into the window. As Bob drew his pistol, he was told to wait until Charley gave the signal.

Zee pointed to a framed motto on the wall "God Bless Our Home" and told Jesse to take it down. Jesse swung a straight chair under the motto. Watching, Charley lifted his hand in signal, at the same time drawing his own gun. Bob put his hand on the door knob, his eyes still on Charley. Jesse was standing on the chair loosening the motto when he heard the click of the door. As he turned, Charley yelled "Now!" and Bob fired. Jesse fell dead.

It took a great deal of persuading by the studio to convince Carradine that he should play the role of Bob Ford. Carradine explained that Jesse James had been his boyhood hero, and that he had always despised Ford more than any other character in history. "I learned," he said, "that a man claiming to be Jesse James in the flesh had made his appearance at several cities throughout the country. If true, then both Bob Ford and myself have been grossly maligned."

According to the studio, Power not only was shot by the very gun which "laid poor Jesse in his grave" but he had the extraordinary privilege of "dying" with Jesse's own boots on. One thing failed to come off—the thoughtful resident of McDonald County failed to sell King the actual guns used by Jesse and Frank James. Assuming that these honest souls were correct, Jesse carried about him at all times, enough firearms to start a munition plant: Jesse's "favorite" Colt, ninety-six Colts, seventy-three derringers, a blunderbuss, two revolutionary muzzle-loading rifles, five shotguns and something that looked like a trench mortar.

VI

EPILOGUE

*"Jesse James took about two hundred thousand dollars out of Missouri, but **Jesse James** brought more than two and a half times that much back."*

Suddenly it was all over. It was as if an earthquake had hit this small rural corner of Missouri Ozarks, but the innocent, unsophisticated friendliness of this area made up for the pandemonium that was left. The whiskers came off. The buggies went back into the barns, the mules went back to the corn patches, and oldtime costumery was returned to the moth balls forever.

Officials estimated that at least 100,000 persons were attracted to McDonald County when the picture was being filmed. Local businessmen believed the visitors spent at least half a million dollars during their stay. Reports circulated that Twentieth Century-Fox studio spent $1,600,000 making the picture. More money flowed into Pineville and Noel than was taken in normally during the course of an entire year.

Staffs at both Pineville and Noel post offices were forced to work overtime taking care of the tremendous increase in mail, including thousands of fan letters for the stars. As the postmaster of Noel said: "It's great stuff for Noel. Used to be when I went to Kansas City, Missouri, people would ask me where I lived. I'd say in Noel, Missouri. They'd say, 'Where's Noel?' But this fall when I go up to Kansas City, when I answer I live in Noel, they'll say, 'You don't say!' "

Wholesale grocers, bread companies, and bottle workers at Joplin were forced to obtain extra trucks to handle the unprecedented demand for foodstuffs and soft drinks. The driver for one bottling company found his orders jumped from 100 to 500 cases in one day. A Pineville school boy sold thirty-three cases of pop during the filming of one scene.

Circulation of newspapers in the area increased by as much as 1,000 percent, and it had been estimated that more than 5,000 copies of a specially printed booklet containing the life history of Jesse and Frank James were sold in Pineville and Noel alone. Professional and free-lance photographers did a land-office business selling pictures of Tyrone Power, Henry Fonda, and other members of the cast. Publicity accorded the region also started something of a real estate boom, and town officials at both Pineville and Noel reported they had received letters from persons seeking to purchase business sites, summer resorts and even farms in the vicinity.

A very mild dissent raised in the general clamor for the Hollywood visit, was that of the editor of the *Benton County Guide,* Bentonville, Arkansas. He wrote:

> Crops not tended;
> Stills run dry.
> Natives want a slice
> Of that Hollywood pie.
> Yet my country
> 'Tis of thee.
> But the Ozarks ain't
> What they used to be.

But then, he was way over in Arkansas. The natives of Missouri made no complaints, neither, in the last analysis, did the movie troupe.

Whatever misunderstandings existed were all slight. In the main, all went well. As the president of the Pineville Chamber of Commerce remarked, "Jesse James took about two hundred thousand dollars out of Missouri, but *Jesse James* brought more than two and a half times that much back."

Between 300 and 400 inhabitants of the county were employed regularly as extras during the filming. Property owners in Pineville and Noel reaped a harvest by turning the yards and pastures into parking lots, and others operated concession stands.

At Noel, where the film stars ate their meals, cafes were crowded from morning until night. Drug stores at both Noel and Pineville were crowded as well. The Shadow Lake dance pavilion, where the stars and crew members went regularly for recreation, was a nightly gathering place for 300 to 400 dancers.

A cross-section of representative inhabitants of the area revealed the natives were highly appreciative of the unprecedented prosperity the motion picture studio had sent them. And, their relations with individual members of the company had been nothing but the friendliest.

The mayor of Pineville said "everybody with the Twentieth Century-Fox *Jesse James* company is O. K. in my books. We got along with them fine. We're glad they came, and we hope they come back again. They are a mighty fine bunch."

A farmer living near Pineville disclosed "that the Twentieth Century-Fox people have given me steady employment by using me and my team of horses during a slack season. All of us farmers have been given extra work helping getting the sets ready. The company came to our aid just when most of us were in need of ready cash to meet our obligations."

The operator of a large general store at Pineville reported "I checked my books and discovered I sold six times as much goods during the month the *Jesse James* company was here than I did during a similar period the year before. The Twentieth Century-Fox company has put our community in better shape financially than it ever has been before."

The wife of a sawmill operator said "the coming of the motion picture people to our community has been a fine thing for everybody. Even we wives have been given a chance to lay up something for a rainy day by working as extras."

One resort owner at Noel reported "it has been a privilege for us to meet such a fine outstanding gentleman as director Henry King and members of his company, and it has been a privilege for us to extend them such courtesies as we would during their stay in our community."

A cafe owner at Pineville remarked "We've fed so many thousands of visitors and members of the *Jesse James* company at my cafe, I've made enough money to pay for all new fixtures, and I've put enough in the bank to buy myself a new home."

One Pineville attorney recalled "that the *Jesse James* company had brought countless thousands of visitors to our community who otherwise would not have come here. We've enjoyed prosperity, the like of which we never knew before, and all the other towns in the Ozarks area also enjoyed some of that same prosperity accommodating the many visitors who had come to see the stars and the actual making of movies."

One lady remembered the hubbub of 1938 with mixed feelings. "I guess there were people from every state in the Union here. I used to watch them standing at the barricades in the hot sun. They would turn so red and finally collapse."

Her husband's drugstore in Pineville was one of the few places of business that stayed open. "One of the big men of the movie company

87

was here at the house," she said. "We were kind of proud of Pineville because we never raised the price of our cokes. They stayed right at five cents. When I told him that, he said that was our mistake. The company expected us to raise prices."

The barber referred to the filming of *Jesse James* as Pineville's one and only boom. "They built that Dixie Belle Saloon. Later that was made into a movie theatre. They boarded over the sidewalks around the whole square." He remembered how hard-working the movie company was. "That's one thing I learned. They put in a good full day, I tell you. They were out and on location by good daylight and worked as long as they had light enough."

Some of the stars got fed up with the attention they received. The barber recalled a story that had been told about Henry Fonda.

"A local man went into a bar in Noel and went up next to Henry Fonda. Henry Fonda turned to him and said, 'What do you want, my autograph?' 'No,' the man replied, 'all I want is to have my beer and get out.'"

One lady was chosen to play the part of the wife of a frontier landowner. At the time, she had three young children who were cast as the landowner's family. "They'd come to pick us up in their big limousines," she recalled. "We were treated real good. They made sure we ate real good."

About the tourists, one lady recalled, "They thought we were cannibals. One woman wanted to know if Henry Fonda learned to chew tobacco from our men. I told her that our men had been taught some things by Henry Fonda."

The company needed absolute quiet. This was difficult with the crowds. "The least little noise and they'd have to shoot again," one lady recalled. "They were out there shooting, and little boys opened bottles of pop. The director said that would sound just like a shotgun in the film."

The crowd of spectators caused problems for Pineville. "If you were on one side of the store you couldn't get to the other side," remarked one merchant. "You couldn't hardly get out of the house. There wasn't any rest. Things rattled all night. Then there was some awfully foolish people, older people, who would say, 'Oh, I touched him! I touched Henry Fonda!' It was disgusting."

Did the children enjoy watching the film stars at work?

"Children didn't have a chance," remarked one lady. "The grown-ups would have suffocated them."

"We have a lot of people who got employment from it," recalled one man, "but it was a headache for us. We had people come and spend a week with us that we hadn't seen for twenty years."

Most of these back country Missourians did not see all of this as a grand opportunity to gouge the rich folks. Of course, there were a few interested in making a fast buck as sight-seers were still being charged, after the film company departed, ten cents a peek at the ground the sojourners from Hollywood had trod. One local genius worked up a flourishing business selling "the actual gourd that Tyrone Power and Henry Fonda had drunk out of" for twenty-five cents a gourd, until his supply had run out.

One farmer whose cabin was used in the picture recalled "there was an old woman who wanted to sit in the swing where Henry Fonda had sat. Then she wanted to sit on the bench where Randolph Scott had sat. I used to get so tired. Another came up to our cabin where they filmed the first scene. She inspected every log in the cabin. She even took a little piece of the chinking."

At the close of the location, director Henry King presented Pineville with all the "props" used during his stay there. The Dixie Belle Saloon presented a rather incongruous appearance, with a swarm of small boys climbing in and out of the windows and swinging from the rafters; and if plans had gone through it would have been turned into the "Dixie Belle Club," incorporated by a group of citizens and operated on a nonprofit basis, where souvenirs could have been purchased and the best meal in southwest Missouri consumed. But this was not to happen.

An auction was arranged by the town to dispose of the lumber and the Dixie Belle Saloon because it obstructed part of the street. It was the hope of city officials that someone would purchase the place and move it to a location where it might be preserved as tourist attraction. That dream never came true. The dirt was removed from the streets by the film company and within a short time the town square had regained its normal appearance. That is, with one exception— the wood awnings erected over the sidewalks throughout the town were found to be splendid additions, and were allowed to remain.

And so, their work completed, the cast and crew of *Jesse James* bid farewell to their new-found friends. All the local girls promised to write Tyrone Power, Henry Fonda, and Randolph Scott, and they, in turn, promised to answer. Nancy Kelly was besieged by requests for autographed photographs to be mailed upon her return to Hollywood, and she replied that she would send a photo to anyone who would write her. Henry Hull, Slim Summerville, J. Edward Bromberg, Brian Donlevy, John Carradine, Donald Meek, Johnnie Russell, and Jane Darwell all were kept busy for hours on end saying goodbye to individual admirers.

Director King handed the Ozarks a real compliment when he said, "We have never shot a picture in a location which has more beautiful scenery, lights, mountains, or shading of green. This country takes to technicolor beautifully, and we are all more than agreeably surprised and delighted.

"We want to take this opportunity of thanking the people of this region in behalf of Twentieth Century-Fox *Jesse James* technicolor troupes for their splendid cooperation, hospitality and generosity, which made our work in your beautiful Ozarks possible."

Henry King, Tyrone Power, and other cast members flew back to Hollywood while technicians returned in a special train. After their arrival in Hollywood, King joined Darryl Zanuck and Nunnally Johnson to edit the film.

Celebrities by the hundreds attended a special two-hour preview in Hollywood, and four granddaughters of Jesse James saw him ride across the movie screen with guns blazing and posses in pursuit.

But when the granddaughters left the theatre, they were shaking their heads. "It may be entertainment, but it isn't Jesse James. Of course, Tyrone Power, as Jesse James, and the other actors were fine, and the color effects were beautiful and the scenes were well directed," continued the granddaughters, "but about the only connection it had with fact was that there once was a man named James and he did ride a horse."

Still skeptical about whether they would like Hollywood's idea of their "Robin Hood," a delegation of forty-four persons from Pineville and Noel attended the premiere showing of the movie in Tulsa as guests of the Orpheum theatre manager and the Chamber of Commerce.

But it wasn't hard to tell as the folks left the movie what they thought. They liked it. Although some of them had never spoken over the radio before, a group of the visitors were interviewed. They knew whose face was under which bonnet in Mrs. Samuel's front yard and whose hand waved good-bye to someone on the train and whose rooster crowed in Mr. Howard's barnyard. Even if one's neighbor merely swished by in a ruffled skirt or dashed through on a horse half a block from the camera, said neighbor was a member of the cast and "did just fine."

"It sure got me," said a young man, "the way they put the thing together. Jesse and Frank plunged over the cliff up at Bagnell dam, landed in the river just below Noel and came out two miles south of town!" A little joke on the public, which he shared with the film company.

This young man didn't act in the picture, but he had his claim to distinction. He handled the box lunch deal—from 125 to 400 every day—with only two cases of food poisoning during the entire two months of scorching weather. He didn't actually say that a film company acted on its stomach, but some such idea was indicated.

A cross-section of the citizenry of the two towns—a hotel keeper, a newspaper man, a school teacher, a housewife, a waitress, a man eating chili, and a small boy on roller skates—when asked how they liked the picture had given the same answer with the same beaming smile: "Fine!"

The mayor of Pineville, remarked "Yes, sir, I know that place; it's out on the knoll behind the town. Know that one, too. They wanted a field with dead trees and corn stalks in it. That's the old Adams place, and I know that man there by the wagon—he's a Pineville man. And say, there's my granddaughter."

One woman saw herself a lot of times but, "it really wasn't much of a thrill—considering how I looked. I had on a baggy old apron and poke bonnet and, well, you get the idea."

The local newspaper editor said, "the color was marvelous, not that it flattered our scenery. We really do have scenery up there. The funniest shot to me was the inside of the newspaper office where the old editor was supposed to be dictating an editorial to a typesetter. If that man could set type as fast as he was supposed to be doing to get that editor's words down in print, then he's got a job coming anywhere he wants to apply. Printers will get plenty of laughs out of that

91

scene.''

"Some of the pictures were very beautiful," said one lady. About the sound track she said, "I know a woman who goes to that movie just to hear the night noises, the frogs and crickets, oh, I love those night noises. That's music to me."

The only diversity of opinion lay in the matter of "who stole the show." Several said Hank Fonda simply walked away with it, that Nancy Kelly turned in by far the best performance "even if she does sort of act with her neck." One was so enthusiastic about Brian Donlevy that he thought the picture "had fallen down a lot" after he had gotten in his dirty work and went back to Hollywood.

John Carradine, that "dirty little coward that shot Mr. Howard," also had his share of staunch supporters. Carradine simply kept them in stitches by such antics as turning up here and there in a trick hat or a linen duster, and sweeping off his fellow actors with a broom every time they stretched out on the grass for a nap.

Was it a big letdown when the movie company left? "I'd call it more of a relief," the barber recalled, "they started August 21 and finished in October. That was the hottest, driest summer we've ever had. The weather didn't interfere with their filming at all. Then after they'd finished the picture, our drought ended. We had the darnedest rain we ever had and it turned cold. October, you know. It's funny, but it just happened that way."

INCOMPLETE BIOGRAPHIES
OF STARS

*These sketches were released
by the publicity department of
Fox to area newspapers prior
to the arrival of the cast.*

HENRY KING

To chronicle the accomplishments of Henry King, ace director at the 20th Century-Fox studios, takes on the hue of seeming exaggeration, so varied and remarkable is the record of what this man has done and can do.

King has been actor, producer, writer and director of some of the finest motion pictures ever made. What is more, nearly all of them have been successes at the box-office. He knows every angle of this highly-specialized and creative business. In the matter of camera action, of motion picture equipment and lighting effects he is looked upon as a master.

To his credit in the field of discovery can be placed the bringing of the late Ernest Torrence, Ronald Colman and Gary Cooper to the screen.

Away from motion pictures, King is one of the best aviators in the country. He operates his own plane and has flown to all parts of the land at frequent intervals. When tired or perplexed from work, he tunes up his ship and soars above the clouds, six, eight, or ten thousand feet above the earth and meditates. He says he has secured some of his best ideas while soloing in the calm of the higher altitudes.

Very definite ideas has this man in the scheme of creating imagination in the form of screen plays. He says, and his career proves it conclusively, that he has never taken into consideration the matter of emolument and the earning of a livelihood. On the contrary, he has fixed an ideal and followed it. Whatever his earnings, they have followed his pursuit of the ideal.

King was born at Christiansburg, high up in the Blue Ridge section of Virginia, on January 24th. His father owned a large plantation and was a railroad attorney. His grandfather, John Howard King, was a first lieutenant under General Robert E. Lee. King confesses that many of his relatives were politicians and that some of them went to Congress. He can truthfully be referred to as of the "F.F.V.", otherwise the First Families of Virginia.

He was educated in the public schools of Riverside and Roanoke in Virginia, and the greatest blow came to the youth when he couldn't go to the University of Virginia because of ebbing family fortunes. His father and mother really wanted him to study for the Methodist ministry, but he had other plans.

King left home when he became of age and went into show business. He toured with stock companies, circuses, vaudeville and burlesque troupes. He eventually became leading man to Anna Boyle, who toured the south in Shakespearean repertoire. He had reached New York and was a lead in Henry W. Savage's production of *Top O' the Morning* when he decided to try out motion pictures. His first work was with the old Lubin company. Later he discovered Baby Marie Osborne and appeared as co-star with her in six pictures, made at the old Pathe studio at Balboa. It was there that he began his career as director. He not only directed, but wrote most of the stories and played the featured roles.

Probably his most unusual achievement was the production of *23½ Hours Leave* a picture that made the entire industry sit up and take notice. Later he went to New York and became the real guiding genius of the new Inspiration Company. He was the executive head and his first production brought stardom and fame to Richard Barthelmess. The picture was *Tol'able David* and it was in this film he gave a tall, gaunt Scotch singer a chance at character work. The player was Ernest Torrence. King next made *Fury* with Barthelmess and then went to Italy and produced *The White Sister* with Lillian Gish as the star. It was in this piece that he brought forth Ronald Colman, who had no previous picture experience. The director went back to Italy again and made *Romola*, with Lillian Gish and her sister, Dorothy.

Returning to the United States he made *Stella Dallas*, with Belle Bennett. Next he made *The Winning of Barbara Worth* and gave Gary Cooper his initial screen opportunity. Following this King directed *The Woman Disputed, She Goes to War* and *Hell's Harbor*.

King explains some of his ideals and theories when he points out that the important thing with him is to know well each character in his pictures before he starts to work. He says if he didn't know his characters he would fail.

Golf, fishing and swimming are favorite pastimes with King, when he is not working or flying his plane. He likes speed and was

Typical scene of Pineville in 1938

Neosho's Kansas City Southern depot became "St. Louis" to depict the start of the St. Louis Midland Railroad between St. Louis and Liberty.

Shadow Lake Resort in Noel, photographed in more recent years. It was a favorite hangout of movie stars during the filming.

Sightseers thronged wherever scenes were to be filmed. Here they crush closely around a railroad baggage car, with Fonda and Power on top, waiting for cameras to roll at the Neosho rail yards.

The air of camaraderie that prevailed on the Missouri location is aptly expressed in the informal shot of Tyrone Power, Nancy Kelly, and Director Henry King strolling gayly to the set.

Tyrone Power

"Jesse James Cabin" on the old Noel-Pineville river road as it appears today.

A recent photo of the old Southwest City railroad station which was used to depict Liberty.

Tyrone Power

King checks Tyrone Power's makeup. With temperatures hovering around one hundred degrees, the entire cast sported red faces.

The iron horse chugging farther and farther West, bringing conflict as well as prosperity into the lives of the simple hardy pioneers, whose lands unscrupulous railroad magnates ruthlessly snatched for right-of-way.

Barshee, representative of the St. Louis Midland Railroad, and his henchmen map out the land they want to acquire.

Barshee applies pressure to an elderly woman and her son.

Barshee and his henchmen eyeing Jesse (out of scene) as Mrs. Samuel pleads with Frank to avoid violence.

Barshee attempts to harm Frank and answers to Jesse.

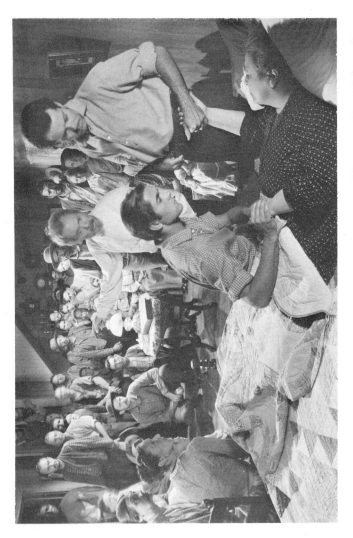

Mrs. Samuel has a heart attack over the excitement of **Barshee**. The Major tells Jesse and Frank that Barshee is planning to return with the sheriff. Jesse and Frank decide to hide out.

Lon Chaney, Jr., Henry Hull awaiting the arrival of Barshee at James Home.

The old Crowder farm as it appeared before it was torn down.

A group of farmers and their wives gather in front of the James home awaiting the arrival of Barshee.

once an amateur automobile race driver. He reads a great deal, and particularly things which give promise of furnishing good motion picture material.

His pet is a famous bull dog with a pedigree.

*****

TYRONE POWER

Tyrone Power, son and namesake of one of the greatest actors in theatrical history, and a beautiful and talented mother, Patia Power, of the stage and radio—before him lies a fascinating future, due to the foresight of Darryl F. Zanuck, production chief of 20th Century-Fox, and his own unquestioned ability as an actor.

Those who have had the pleasure of meeting Tyrone Power talk of his charm and his poise. He had the ease of manner, the culture and graciousness for which producers and director's are forever searching. He receives one with the cordiality and sincere interest that gives impetus to conversation.

Yet...three years ago (1935) Hollywood turned its back nonchalantly on the handsome brown-eyed youth. In the language of the studios, Hollywood gave Tyrone Power a "kick in the pants" and a "slap in the face" and sent him on his tortuous route to Broadway success on the stage.

Just how much obstacles play in the game of building a career is difficult to determine. This much is apparent, however: No man has ever risen to greatness without being forced to hurdle some obstacle, or to overcome some handicap.

In the case of youthful Tyrone Power, it was his distinguished ancestry, more than any one thing, that proved a handicap, insofar as Hollywood was concerned. Even on Broadway it was an obstacle, for a time, to be overcome in establishing himself as an individual...as an actor by right of his own shining talent.

Tyrone's ancestral trees on both sides of the family bear many famous names. On the paternal side the roots of the tree are imbeded in the soil of Ireland, and in England; on the maternal side, in France and America. When the fighting blood of such a foursome mingles and flows through the heart of a courageous youth, it is a combination hard to beat.

Success, apparently, is in the blood. There are some humans whom Fate can never keep down. They march forward and take by divine right the best the world affords. But success, after all, is nothing more than courage...the will to fight and keep on when everything seems darkest.

Of such stuff is young Tyrone Power made. You will see for yourself as his story unfolds.

Tyrone Power, 20th Century-Fox star, is the third of his family to bear the name. The first was his great-grandfather, named after County Tyrone, the homeland of the Power family, and his son, Harold Power, was the father of Tyrone, the second, who, in turn, named his only son, the subject of this sketch, Tyrone. Harold Power, during his life time, was one of England's famous concert pianists. Young Tyrone's father was born in London.

Tyrone's mother, with whom he lives in Hollywood, was born in Indianapolis, Indiana. She is an exceptionally beautiful and talented woman. Her voice is recognized by critics as one of the most expressive and flexible on the stage and radio. Her eyes and her smiles, all embracing, she gave to her son and their duplication of his mother's are among his outstanding assets.

Her family name is Reaume. She was given the name of Emma at birth but at the time she married Mr. Power in 1912, she had her name changed legally to Patia, and as Patia Power she is known throughout the theatrical and radio world.

Tyrone Power, the third, was born one bright spring day—May 5, 1914—at 5:30 o'clock in the afternoon, in Cincinnati, Ohio, in the home of his Grandmother Reaume, 2112 Fulton Avenue.

In speaking of that eventful occasion, Mrs. Power said:

"Tyrone was a most considerate baby. I was appearing with Mr. Power in Shakespearean roles during this parental period, and I worked on the stage until within two months of his birth. Incidentally, consideration for others has always been one of my boy's outstanding characteristics."

When Tyrone was between two and three months of age, his parents were signed under contract to Famous Players and worked in silent pictures in and about New York. When the baby was a year old they were transferred to Hollywood, under contract to Selig pictures.

When Tyrone was seventeen months of age, his sister, Ann, was born in Hollywood. She is now Mrs. Leslie Tyrer and lives in Honolulu.

Shortly afterwards Mr. Power was engaged to play in the New York stage production of *Chu Chin Chow*. The family moved to New York and established a home there.

Little Tyrone, who was a frail child until his seventh year, could not combat with the rigors of an eastern winter. Patia Power and the two children returned to California, going directly to San Diego.

By that time the first of the American Expeditionary Forces had landed in France. Mrs. Power provided a home for herself and the children, secured a dependable nurse for them and entered into the work of the American Red Cross. Troops for overseas service and for coast defense were mobilizing in and about San Diego harbor. Realizing the need for entertainment in the various camps, Patia Power, always resourceful organized a branch of the Stage Women's War Relief, a unit of the Red Cross. She formed a little stock company, the Power Players, and, for the duration of the war and through the demobilization period, she staged plays, vaudeville shows and concerts for the men at arms in the recreation halls and huts. She received national recognition for her valiant service.

In the meantime, little Tyrone played on the sands of Coronado beach, gaining in health and strength in the sunshine, with his sister, Ann.

When her war work was completed, Patia Power moved with the children to Alhambra, in the sun-kissed San Gabriel valley, near Los Angeles. She had been engaged to play the leading feminine role, Senora Josefa Yorba, in John Steven McGroarty's celebrated Mission Play, staged annually at old Mission San Gabriel. She played the part, which, for its emotional appeal was the high spot in the production, for five seasons.

One might say that Tyrone was literally brought up on the Mission Play, as a child. His mother's dressing-room was his playroom and also his classroom during the run of the play every season. He was always asking Mr. McGroarty when he and Ann would be "growed up enough" to be real actors in the production.

It was a red-letter day in his life, when at the age of seven years, Mr. McGroarty assigned him to the role of Pablo, a neophyte of the Franciscan padres. It was his first role in any theatre.

Strangely enough the older Tyrone Power, during his residence in Hollywood, played the role of Father Junipero Serra, founder of the

California missions, in the McGroarty play when the boy was two years of age. Mrs. Power took the children to see their father. Ann was a babe in arms. It was the first time either had even been inside of a theatre.

Mr. McGroarty was so impressed with young Tyrone's talent in the Pablo role that, when he decided to stage his next play, *La Golondrina* he gave the boy, then seven, an important role. The piece, dealing with early California life, was staged in the Mission theatre also.

Edwin Schallert, dean of Los Angeles dramatic critics, reviewing *La Golondrina* in the Los Angeles *Times*, said:

"Among those cited for masterful performances is Master Tyrone Power, especially, for the miniature hit."

In 1923, Patia Power was engaged by the Schuster-Martin School of the Drama, in Cincinnati, to take over the chair of voice and dramatic expression. With the children she moved to the Ohio city and again established a home.

Tyrone, always a slender child was restored to splendid health during the years in California. He was enrolled, with his sister, at the Sisters of Mercy Academy, in the third grade. When Tyrone reached the sixth grade he was sent to St. Xavier Academy where he completed his elementary school work. From there he went to the preparatory school of the University of Dayton, in Dayton, Ohio. This was the boy's first experience in being away from home. Like all the other schools he attended, it was parochial under the supervision of the Brothers of Mary. He spent two semesters at Dayton and then returned to Cincinnati and entered Purcell high school, also a Brothers of Mary institution. He graduated from Purcell in 1931, at the age of seventeen.

During school years he took an active part in dramatics, studied the speech arts under his mother's supervision, and played the lead in the senior class play the year he graduated. The play was *Officer 666*. Tyrone also "went to business" during those adolescent years. When he was fifteen he worked as a drug clerk and when he was sixteen he ushered at the Orpheum when not in school.

When he graduated from Purcell there was a family conference relative to sending the boy to college. He persuaded his parents to permit him to take a practical course in Shakespearean roles on the spoken stage, rather than go to college. He wanted more than anything in the world to be not only an actor, but a good actor. And that is his ideal today in his screen work...but, now, he not only wants to be a good actor, he wants to be one of the best.

Mr. Power had been engaged for a short season in Shakespearean repertoire in the Chicago Civic Auditorium for the early fall of 1931. Others in the notable cast were Fritz Leiber, William Faversham and Helen Mencken.

He decided to give his son the opportunity he craved. With that in mind, he took Tyrone to a quiet summer retreat in Quebec. There during the summer of 1931, under the direction of his father, recognized as one of the greatest actors in theatrical history, the boy was given intensive study and rehearsals in the roles, small though they were, that he was to delineate in the Chicago season. It was a summer for young Tyrone never to be forgotten...a priceless memory of a beloved father.

The first production in which Tyrone appeared as a professional actor was *The Merchant of Venice* and he played an old man, friend of the Doge of Venice, impersonated by his illustrious father.

And...in that first professional appearance, Tyrone came as near to a tragic ending as any human would ever care to be!

As part of the action of his part, Fritz Leiber, playing the title role, picked up a huge knife of the period. While gesticulating with it, inadvertently it slipped from his grasp, flying across the stage with terrific force. It passed so close to Tyrone's cheek that it fanned his hair! It stuck in the scenery at his back almost up to the hilt! The boy, poised, as always remained in character and perfectly calm. His father, sitting nearby in a chair, stiffened clenched the sides of the chair and breathed in a whisper:

"My God! son, are you hurt?"

Leiber had practically collasped, fearing the worse. The audience, for several minutes went through an emotional upheaval.

Thus was Tyrone Power's introduction to the stage!

At the conclusion of the Chicago season Mr. Power was engaged to go to Hollywood to play the starring role in Paramount's spoken production of *The Miracle Man*. Tyrone went to Hollywood also, as he had been promised a small part in the play. Mrs. Power and Ann remained in their Cincinnati home and Mrs. Power continued with her work at the dramatic school. Father and son were living together in the film capital.

Work on *The Miracle Man* was under way when Mr. Power was taken ill on the set. But, trouper that he was, he made no complaint and worked until midnight, when he collapsed. Tyrone was called and took him home. At four o'clock that morning—December 30, 1931, he died in his son's arms.

Patia Power and Ann came at once from Cincinnati to be with Tyrone. The small part he was to have in *The Miracle Man* did not materialize. He began to hunt for work. He did the usual thing, making the rounds of the casting offices and the agents' sanctums. All turned deaf ears to the boy. He had no opportunity to "display his wares." If he were given an appointment, it was because some oldster wished to reminisce about his father, recalling when they had seen him as Brutus in *Julius Caesar*; or Abu Hasan in *Chu Chin Chow*; or Sir Anthony absolute in *The Rivals*; or a dozen other notables characterizations, while the boy listened attentively, but inwardly realizing that he was up against the biggest obstacle to date.

Tyrone, with his mother and sister, moved to Santa Barbara, where they became actively identified with the Community Theatre, the boy studying, always, to perfect his work, under his mother's direction. When he was not working in a little theatre play, he was in Hollywood trying to get a "break."

After trying for nearly two years to get by the casting offices to Hollywood..."almost getting something, but never quite"...Tyrone decided to go to New York City and try to make the grade on the spoken stage. He sallied forth with his mother's blessing and the good wishes of his friends, determined to "fight it out."

That decision changed the whole course of his career.

En route to New York he stopped off in Chicago to see some of his friends. The Century of Progress Exposition was in full swing and he was engaged for the Circuit Theatre productions. He ventured into radio and landed, happily, on the same program, *Grand Hotel*, with Don Ameche. The charming friendship between the two young men was established at that time and renewed with much happiness when they met again at 20th Century-Fox. Incidentally, both Don and Tyrone made scores of tests for the role of Jonathan Blake in *Lloyds of London*, with Tyrone winning the coveted role in the final test. They appeared together in *Love Is News*.

Tyrone did quite a bit of radio work while in Chicago, working in dramatic plays and in the religious hour sponsored by Sears-Roebuck. It was not all "sweetness and light" for him during that period, but it was experience and he was learning something constructive as time passed.

Toward the close of 1934, which proved a memorable year for Tyrone, he was engaged to play the part of Freddie in *Romance* produced by Luther Greene at the Blackstone Theatre, Chicago, with the brilliant Eugenie Lenotovitch starred. The piece ran eight weeks.

At his conclusion Tyrone decided it was time to be on his way to his destination—New York—and, he hoped—Broadway.

Then began another whirl at the casting managers' offices. He budgeted his savings and allowed himself five dollars per week upon which to live and provide for himself generally.

His first "break" came in the form of a comfortable sleeping room, rent-free, through the hospitality of the gracious Michael Strange, an old family friend, former wife of John Barrymore.

His first real behind-the-scenes "break" in his New York experience came through the courtesy of Helen Mencken, the noted stage star, whom he had met during the Shakespearean season in Chicago.

She phoned Guthrie McClintic, eminent stage director and husband of Katherine Cornell, that when young Tyrone Power sought him for an interview, it would be to his advantage to see the boy. She knew his parents and she knew the youngster had talent—lots of it.

Tyrone wanted very much to see Katherine Cornell, then appearing in *Flowers of the Forest*. He did not have the money to spend on a theatre ticket, so he went to Stanley Gilkey, manager of Miss Cornell, to ask for a pass. He did not have to ask. Mr. Gilkey gave him a pair of passes and Mr. McClintic gave him a couple of parts to take home and read.

Tyrone was so excited for such an "in" with the theatrical great that, after seeing *Flowers of the Forest* that night, he remained up until dawn writing his mother and sister all the details of his thrilling experience.

By request he went back to Guthrie McClintic's office the next day. He was assigned to understudy two players, one of them being Burgess Meredith the leading man. Tyrone did not have an opportunity to appear in either role on the stage during the season, but he spent his time in observing and absorbing the work and the technique of the artists in the cast.

When the Cornell season closed Tyrone went to a summer stock company at West Falmouth, Mass. In his pocket was a contract to play the role of Benvolio, friend of Romeo, in Katherine Cornell's production of *Romeo and Juliet* at the Martin Beck Theatre, New York, in the fall.

By the time he had appeared in a few plays at West Falmouth, notably in *On Stage* in which he made a distinct hit in the role of Jerry, the Hollywood scouts, no less, were on his trail—on his heels, literally, as a matter of fact.

Tyrone, however, wanted to learn more about acting through spoken stage experience. He was convinced, after removing many obstacles from his path to Broadway, that when he did go to Hollywood—and he always felt he would, when the time was right—he wanted "to land, not to creep."

The tryout of *Romeo and Juliet* was held in Baltimore. Patia Power was there to see her boy in his first Broadway production. How she reacted to that momentous night is best told in her own words:

"I was pleased with the way Tyrone held up his part. He really gave excellent support to the more experienced players—gave them line for line—and never let them down once. I was really proud of his work, both as a mother and as an instructor. When we talked it over afterwards I impressed upon him how much work he must do in order to keep up to the high standard he had set in the tryout."

After the run of *Romeo and Juliet*, Tyrone was engaged again by Katherine Cornell to play the part of de Ponlengey in her production of *St. Joan,* at the Martin Beck Theatre, New York, February, 1936.

By this time, 20th Century-Fox had made a test of Tyrone. It was screened by Darryl F. Zanuck in Hollywood. With a keen and uncanny sense of seeing beyond what the screen unfolds, and with the ability to visualize players in parts he has in mind for the future, the great producer signed Tyrone to a seven-year contract under the 20th Century-Fox banner.

So, now, at the age of twenty-three, Tyrone Power is on his way to the cinema heights. For those who wish to know various details...

He is six feet tall; weighs 155 pounds. He is a handsome youth with dark brown hair and luminous brown eyes. He is a thoroughbred in all the name implies. He is a distinctive addition to the screen's roster of eminently worthwhile players.

He is not married. Prefers blondes. Has no favorite type of girl, but says he will know her when he sees her.

He believes in hunches. Follows them. He followed a hunch the day he went to ask for the pass to Katherine Cornell's show.

His favorite flower is the white carnation. His mother says when he was even a tiny baby a white carnation was ever a source of delight to him. His favorite superstition is whistling in the dressing-room. His greatest fear is that of being shut in...as in a cave or a mine...claustrophobia.

Among the classic authors he prefers Hugo, and Shakespeare is his favorite classical playwright. Of the moderns, he prefers Maxwell Anderson. His favorite historical character is Cyrano de Bergerac.

His favorite classical orchestration is *Tales in the Vienna Woods*; favorite classical painter, Van Gogh; favorite illustrator, Petty; favorite modern painter, Grant Wood; favorite modern author, Thorne Smith, favorite play, *Ethan Frome*.

Reads incessantly...anything that is interesting and constructive and to keep in touch with contemporary magazines and likes to read the *Reader's Digest*.

His favorite color is blue...any shade of blue. His favorite fruit is the avocado...very fond of them.

He is especially fond of outdoors sports and is a football fan. Always wanted to play football when in school and would go out every season for a tryout but did not make the team "because he was too skinny...just a bean-pole as a boy."

His hobby is amateur photography with a 16 mm. camera. He swims, plays tennis and rides horseback when not engaged at the studio.

He says if he should leave Hollywood he would return to New York and the stage...and...perhaps do some writing, a talent in which he excels in a measure almost paralled with his acting ability.

*****

TYRONE POWER

What there is of my life thus far is, like Caesar's Gaul, divided into three parts—early childhood, the pre-Hollywood and the current Hollywood periods. Of the first I remember nothing. The latter is still too fresh and hectic to be catalogued as "memories." The pre-Hollywood, which ended just a year and a half ago, really starts with my first remembered after-dinner "sit still periods." My sister and I would have to remain sitting at the dinner table for fifteen minutes after we had eaten, during which mother would combine this lesson in poise with one in diction. I was a very nervous and flighty youngster, which was one of the reasons mother tried this method of keeping me calm and giving me something to work on.

The first big moment in my life was when I was given my first part in the Mission Play at San Gabriel, California. Mother and father were playing in it, and as they needed a youngster of about seven for a small role, I drew it. It all seemed so natural for me to go in for acting. All of my parents' friends who came to the house were theatrical people, and typical of their kind, they all talked shop. Even before I understood what half of the words meant, I was thoroughly conversant with theatrical lingo. But it was a bit scary getting up before an audience for the first time. Beside my parents there was one other person who helped me greatly at that time. He was Charles C. Hardee, who was not only stage manager but played a big role in the production. A few months ago one of the extras on the set of *In Old Chicago*, came up and greeted me very cordially. It was Charles C. Hardee whom I had not met since I made my debut at the age of seven. Hardee's help at that time was instrumental in persuading John Steven McGroarty to put me in another outdoor play, *La Golondrina*.

When I was nine, mother moved back to Cincinnati, my birthplace, where my sister Ann and I went to school. It was after I completed the sixth grade at St. Xavier Academy that I got my first taste of living away from home. I was sent to the parochial prep school for the University of Dayton in Dayton, Ohio. Later, at Purcell High

School in Cincinnati I got my first lead in a play. The year I graduated, I was given the lead in *Officer 666*, the senior class play.

I was seventeen then, and therefore thought I knew more than I did when I reached the ripe old age of twenty-one. My parents wanted me to go to college. I held out for starting on my stage career immediately. I still didn't think there was any other profession for me in the world. True, I had done some work during summer vacations, but that didn't mean anything more than a way to keep active and pick up a few pennies. For a while I jerked sodas in a corner drug store. That was where I met my first big heart throb and my first information about the movies via the fan magazines. The heart throb, whose name I did know, was a girl who used to come into the store occasionally. I secretly worshipped her, but didn't dare ever approach her. I always hoped that when I was sent out on deliveries, which was also part of my duties, that one of them would be to her house. It never was. That romance was born to blush unseen and unknown to the lady in question. During dull periods at the soda fountain, I used to read all of the fan magazines and wonder if the movie stars pictured in them lived like other mortals and how they labored through life under the gobs of glamor with which they were invested.

To get back to my decision not to go to college, a compromise was reached by father offering to take me for the summer to a country house in Quebec. There I went through an intensive course in Shakespeare. Father trained me like a drill sergeant. We would read plays, taking different parts, interpret them and analyze characters and readings. I guess the idea was to either get me thoroughly fed up on the idea, but I loved it. In fact, that summer proved to be the most valuable bit of training I had ever received. When it became evident that I was determined to turn professional in as short a time as possible, father took me with him to Chicago where he was engaged for a short season of Shakespearean drama at the Chicago Civic Auditorium, season of Fall 1931. In the cast were also Fritz Leiber, William Faversham and Helen Mencken. My first production was *The Merchant of Venice*, in which I played an old man, friend of the Doge of Venice, the latter part played by my father. In that play I had my narrowest escape. As part of his action, Fritz Leiber, as Shylock, was to pick up and brandish a huge knife. In a violent movement, the knife slipped from his grasp and whizzed my head so close that I felt the wind of it on my cheek. When it struck up to the hilt in the scenery, I could see my father stiffen and clench the sides of the chair in which he was sitting. I shall never forget the concern in his whisper, "My God! son are you hurt?" Leiber almost collapsed, and the situation was not lost on the audience. But imbued with all the novice's rapture over the "show must go on" tradition, I carried on in true trouper fashion. At the end of the act, I got the jitters when I thought about now close that knife came to me, but I didn't dare tell father about it.

I may be technically in error when I refer to all of this as my pre-Hollywood period. I did have a try at Hollywood during this time, but as I didn't have any luck, it just doesn't count. It was shortly after my Chicago experience in Shakespeare that father died in the middle of production on *The Miracle Man* at Paramount Studios. I wanted and needed work, but the rounds of the Hollywood casting offices proved fruitless. They admitted me and would talk to me on account of my father's name which I bore, but the conversation was mostly about how great an actor my father was. When I got them around to the job situation, that was a different matter altogether. We went to live in Santa Barbara for a while where I joined a little theatre group, playing in several plays at a tiny salary. Between plays I would come down to Hollywood and tackle the casting directors, but it was a hopeless job. Finally, I did get a break. Universal was about to make a picture called *Tom Brown of Culver*, starring Tom Brown. I got a little part in it, with a promise of a contract and more work. I got a flat $500 for my work throughout the picture—but no contract and no further work. Two years had gone by since father died, and I was getting nowhere fast.

That was when I decided that it was high time I got to New York and make my onslaught on Broadway. On the way, I stopped off in Chicago to renew acquaintance with some old friends. Things were booming in Chicago then, what with the Century of Progress Exposition. One of the first friends I met asked me if I wanted a job. I hadn't had a job for so long that I accepted without asking what sort of work it was and how much it paid. Ironically enough, I was to work in a show at the Exposition where the paid admissions are shown how movies are made in Hollywood. The only trouble was that there weren't enough paid admissions, and salaries were quite often indefinitely delayed. It was during that period that I first met Don

Ameche, one of the biggies in radio. I got occasional radio jobs, and got to know Don that way. My opinion of him as one swell fellow was confirmed when we later worked in pictures together. Anyhow, it was a radio job which drove me out of Chicago. I got a call to report on Sunday morning at a certain station. Came fifteen minutes before broadcast time, and no one had yet offered to let me look at the script I was to do. When I asked for it I was offered the comic supplement of the Sunday paper. The job was to read the funny papers over the radio. That evening, I boarded a train for New York.

It didn't take me long to find out that casting directors and producers on Broadway are the same as they are in Hollywood. They granted me an interview when my name was sent in, talked about what a great actor my father was, but regretted that they had nothing to offer me. Stanley Gilkey, Katharine Cornell's manager, struck me as a very tough customer to tackle. I didn't even dare ask him for a job. I went to ask him for a pass to Miss Cornell's show, but before I could say anything he offered me the job as Burgess Meredith's understudy in *Flowers of the Forest* and gave me a couple of tickets to see the show that night so that I could get acquainted with it. That moment in Gilkey's office stands out as one of the big thrill moments of my life. I had made Broadway!

Hollywood came shortly after that, but the thrill was not as great. I made a screen test without even a vague hope of getting into pictures. I had already had my experience in trying to crash Hollywood. That test was terrible, and I didn't even try to kid myself. Even Darryl F. Zanuck who looked at it in Hollywood thought it was so terrible that he ordered another made before he would order my candidacy thrown out. The second one turned the trick. The rest of the story is too much of a surrealist conglomeration in my mind to even attempt to be coherent about it.

*****

NANCY KELLY

In the cool gloom of a theatre in the heart of New York, on an autumn morning that was to be momentous in the life of a certain young girl, John Golden, the great producer of stage successes, settled wearily back in his chair.

Golden was listening to ambitious young beauties who were trying out for the part of Blossom, Gertrude Lawrence's daughter, in Rachel Crothers' play, *Susan and God*, a vehicle destined to be one of the great hits of the 1938 season on Broadway.

The parade of pretty ingenues with their cultivated, dramatic-school voices, went on and on. Golden was weary. None of them had given evidence of that exciting spark which marks histrionic genius. Restlessly, the producer stirred. He reached for his hat. Sitting near him, Miss Crothers whispered:

"Just a minute, Mr. Golden. You're going to find that your wait was worthwhile, after all."

A tall, slender brown-haired girl walked, then, across the bright and empty stage. She seemed to fill that stage with a vernal charm, a haunting wistfulness. Grace was hers, and beauty, too; and, that indefinable quality called magnetism.

And when she spoke, her voice echoed like lute music; its nuances were strangely lovely; there was about it a rare and mellow sound that endowed all her words with euphony.

Golden nodded.

"That's the girl!" he cried.

That girl was Nancy Kelly, a few months later to be hailed by blase Manhattan critics as the most refreshing actress to tread the Broadway stage in many a season....as the youngster most likely to attain definite stardom in whatever medium she might choose, the cinema or the legitimate theatre.

Because he is ever alert to the possibility of finding a new and glamorous personality about which to weave the magic cloak of fame, Darryl F. Zanuck, 20th Century-Fox vice-president in charge of production, acted quickly when news of Nancy Kelly's talent and beauty and charm reached him, out in Hollywood.

He ordered a screen test. The test was rushed to him by air express. Zanuck, the "star maker," viewed the test and reacted even as John Golden had when Nancy Kelly stepped on the barren stage and began to read her lines as Blossom.

"Sign her!" was his cryptic order.

So Nancy Kelly very presently was on her way to Hollywood...seventeen years old and already on the threshold of a career so bright with promise that she is today one of the most talked-about enthused-about newcomers in Cinemaland.

When Nancy Kelly, on a radiant day in May, stepped from the Santa Fe Super Chief to face a battery of still cameras and a chattering squadron of newspapermen who popped questions like a machine gun barrage, she was setting foot on California earth for the first time.

Yet, despite this, and despite the tenderness of her years, she really was a veteran of motion pictures, already; for she had to her credit no less than fifty-two parts in pictures.

These, however, all were made in the East—on Long Island, and Nancy appeared in them as a child star—appearing opposite such renowned players as Warner Baxter, Jean Hersholt, Gloria Swanson and many another.

Her first act, upon arriving in Hollywood, was to telephone Baxter, with whom she played in *The Great Gatsby* twelve years ago, when Nancy was an elfin tot of five. Baxter, probably the most perennially popular star in Hollywood history, and Nancy, the little-girl-of-not-so-long-ago, lost little time in arranging a reunion, which was as joyous and as exhilarating to them as mountain breezes.

Great things are expected of the present-day Nancy Kelly. But let us peer, for a moment, into the Nancy Kelly of other years, the wistful child who endeared herself to millions.

Let us even go back to the romance of Jack Kelly, a handsome young Irishman who loved the theatrical business, and Nan Walsh, a blue-eyed colleen who was making a name for herself on the stage.

When a Kelly meets a Walsh and says, "Faith, darlin', I'll love you till the lakes of Killarney are dry and the sun no longer shines on the emerald fields of old Ireland," they get married; which is what Jack Kelly and Nan Walsh did.

Mrs. Samuel is dead. Barshee had thrown a bomb into the house believing Jesse and Frank were there.

Zee goes to the hideout and tells Jesse and Frank about the death of their mother. Jesse vows vengeance.

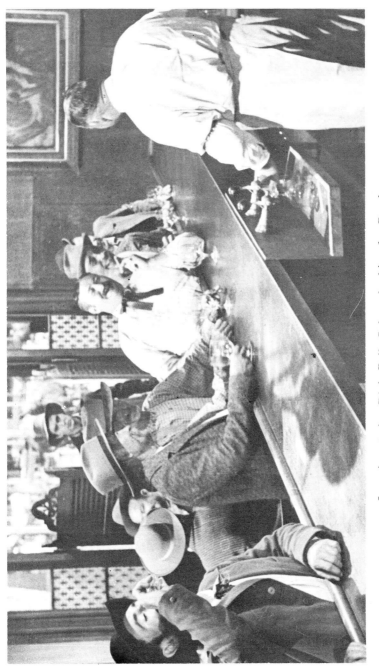

Jesse is entering Dixie Belle Saloon looking for Barshee.

Jesse aims at Barshee.

Barshee pleads for life, but to no avail.

Jesse vows to make the railroad pay by robbing it.

Jesse leaps on train.

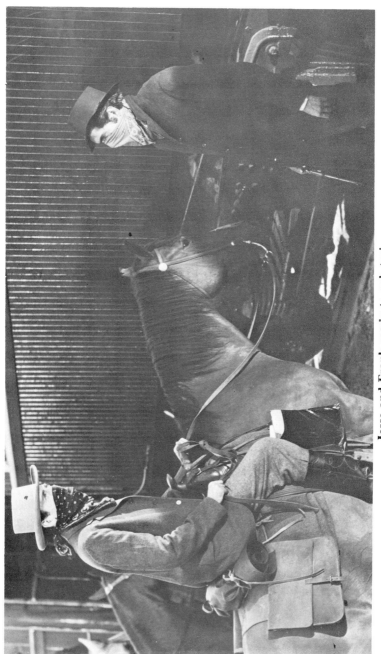

Jesse and Frank ready to rob train.

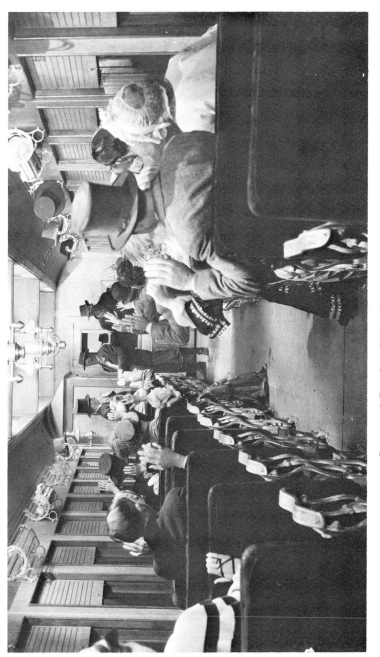

Jesse and Frank robbing the passengers.

Jesse pauses for a rest after the holdup.

Zee pleads with Jesse and Frank to stop before it is too late.

After robbing a bank, Jesse and Frank elude a posse, but Jesse's horse stumbles.

Mill Creek Baptist Church where Jesse and Zee are married.

Jesse and Zee being married.

Jesse and Zee leave the church.

Newlyweds Jesse and Zee leave the church in a carriage as Bob Ford and Frank James look on.

Nan retired from the stage and they went to the quiet, old-fashioned city of Lowell, Mass., to live. It was in Lowell, on a day of wild winds and bluster that seemed somehow appropriate to the delighted pride of the brand-new father, that Nancy Kelly, brown-eyed like her dad, was born. That was March 25, 1921.

Jack and Nan Kelly were big city people. Lowell was all right for awhile, but, when Nancy was two months old, they harkened to the siren call of the metropolis and moved to New York, where Jack set himself up in the theatre ticket brokerage business.

It was inevitable that Nan, an actress of undoubted ability herself, should look for signs of histrionic talent in her first-born. Nancy was only four years old when those signs showed themselves to such a degree that advertising agencies began to clamor for the youngster's services as a model.

Likewise, she was an incredibly beautiful and healthy child. A committee of physicians pronounced her "100 per cent physically perfect." Before she was five she was known as "America's most photographed child." You couldn't pick up a magazine without seeing Nancy's likeness, staring wistfully or smilingly, as the case might be, from an elaborate advertisement of some kind or other.

Her fame spread far and wide, so it was definitely logical that Mrs. Kelly should receive a call from Paramount's Long Island studios, to the effect that Gloria Swanson would be interested in seeing Nancy with a view to obtaining the child's services in *The Untamed Lady*.

Nancy came; Gloria saw, and was conquered. Thus, at the age of four, her motion picture career was launched. Picture followed picture in rapid sequence. Paramount, First National, the old Fox company, all availed themselves of bright-eyed Nancy's unique talent. She worked with Richard Dix, Herbert Brenon and Rudy Vallee. Among the major successes in which she appeared were *Say It Again, Glorifying the American Girl* and *The Girl on the Barge*, in which she played the daughter of lovable, benign Jean Hersholt, who, like Baxter, now is a 20th Century-Fox star, and who joined Warner in welcoming the young actress, all grown up, to the big lot between the mountains and the sea in Westwood, California.

When F. Scott Fitzgerald's *The Great Gatsby* was being filmed, with Baxter in the title role, an affection between the star and the child began, and, with Mrs. Kelly's beaming approval, Warner took Nancy on many a gay journey around and about in Little Old New York, to the Aquarium, the Bronx Zoo, Coney Island, Central Park for long walks amid the greenery and canoeing on the shimmering lake, and even to the Algonquin and the famous restaurants of the day, where Warner gravely introduced Nancy to his adult compadres as "my future leading lady." It was not beyond the bound of possibilty that Baxter's pleasant quip of that bygone day may become a reality.

When Nancy reached the ripe, old age of six, her mother and father decided that, even though fame and fortune were hers, the time had come to concentrate upon her education; for, gifted with that second sight which often seems to be inherent in daughters of the Emerald Isle, Mrs. Kelly believed firmly that her daughter was not to be merely a "wonder child," but was to go on to lasting heights and a lifetime career in her chosen profession.

So, under the tutelage of the nuns of the Immaculate Conception Academy in New York, little Miss Kelly began pursuit of the noun and the pronoun, the multiplication table, and the things that people put in textbooks. Later, she was enrolled at St. Lawrence Academy on Long Island, and, when she reached the "teen" age, she became a member of the student body at the swank, exclusive Bentley School for Girls.

There were intervals when, temporarily, Nancy was permitted to desert the classroom for the stage. One such time was when she appeared in Charles Hopkins' production of the delicately whimsical Milne play, *Give Me Yesterday*. At these times, a private tutor bided her time in Nancy's dressing room backstage, ready to see to it that the youngster's education was uninterrupted by the footlights.

There came, as it must to all children, the "awkward age." Nancy had an idea about that. "Mother," she said, very seriously, "why don't I hide behind the microphone until I'm over being awkward?"

So, radio it was. Nancy became the first and only ingenue on the *March of Time* program. Too, she was the first dramatic star of her age on the air. Dialects were strictly one of her fortes. Via the "mike," she did "everything from Freddie Bartholomew to Princess Juliana in childbirth," she says. She was, as can be seen at the well-known glance, the busiest child actress on radio when she got the call for the part in *Susan and God* on the stage—the part that was the most coveted of all ingenue roles on Broadway in the 1937-38 season, and the part that was to win her the long-term contract with 20th Century-Fox.

In the meantime, Nancy wasn't the only member of the amazing clan of Kelly who was doing things theatrically in the grand manner. Her brother, Jack, Jr., 10, was appearing in five Hollywood plays, the latest of which is the rollicking *Schoolhouse on the Lot*. Jack, Junior, also supported Ethel Barrymore in the ill-fated "Yankee Doodle" and got himself a thorough grounding in Shakespeare by appearing with Maurice Evans in that distinguished actor's interpretations of the immortal works of the quondam Bard of Avon. Little sister, Carole E., 6, also is on the stage, and it will be no time at all, says the Kellys, *mere et pere*, when the baby of the family, Clement, 3, will be doing his bit to glorify the American stage—with Hollywood just around the corner.

Having grown up in a sizeable family, Nancy, despite all that nonsense about stage children being a bit too adult in their approach to life, remains very much of a normal girl, save in certain cultural phases of her interesting background.

Thus, she is extremely fond of sports. Slim as a Dryad, and as graceful, too, she is an excellent swimmer, and has her eye on a few of those shiny medals which she hears are to be had in and around Hollywood for aquatic skill. She rides horseback, too, and though most of her equestrian activities have taken place on such polite bridle paths as Central Park's, she's anxious to get into a Western saddle on board a Western cayuse and find out for herself about all this "home, home on the range business." A golfer boasting a magnificent set of matched irons, she shoots in the high 80's.

Turning to her preferences in belles—lettres, they are, to say the least, remarkable for a girl of seventeen summers. For instance she is addicted to reading Chaucer in the original Old English. Will Shakespeare, of course, she has read through and through. Because she is gifted in the use of the French language, she reads, in French, De Maupassant, Dumas *pere* and Dumas *fils*, Voltaire, Proust, and Zola.

Nancy, with characteristic intensity, currently is studying music, and she expects to develop her pleasing soprano voice to an extent enabling her to be a genuine singing star.

Nancy's principal hobby is the collecting of "little things." She owns, in miniature, a tremendous collection including ships, dogs, knives, horses, and the like. Her most precious possession at the moment is a bracelet of 52 charms, a present to Nancy from Gertrude Lawrence, when the lovely Miss Kelly left the cast of *Susan and God* to come to Hollywood. She likes, too, "bracelets that make noises," and has an extensive array of those odd articles.

Her favorite play is *The Sea Gull.* Her favorite motion picture is Warner Baxter's *In Old Arizona* which she saw thirty-two times, and her favorite actor is that same Warner Baxter. Her own favorite role is that of Blossom in *Susan and God.*

Nancy's greatest ambition, simply but vividly expressed, is to "live up to what my mother expects of me." She adds: "I suppose all girls are fortunate in their mothers, but I do believe that I've the most remarkable mother in the whole world, and without her I'd be lost." Yes, Mrs. Kelly accompanied Nancy to Hollywood, where they dwell in a dainty little home with chintz curtains that sway insouciantly in the pleasant breezes, and brand-new furniture, which they had a wonderful time selecting.

There's hardly anything that Nancy's afraid of; but she *is* afraid of high places, and she avoids lofty buildings as she would a plague.

As for superstitions, she's jittery about just three things: (a) whenever she thinks she's getting a wee bit conceited, she knocks on wood; (b) she absolutely refuses to be a party to the lighting of three cigarettes from the same match, and (c) those wild horses you hear so much about couldn't force her to walk under a ladder.

The gardenia—and there is a delicate, gardenia-like quality about Nancy—is her favorite flower. Chaucer, as we have seen, is her preference in classical authors, and Chekhov wins Nancy's nod among the classical playwrights. Her favorite classical orchestration is Beethoven's *Moonlight Sonta* and Rembrandt is the Old Master who most appeals to her. As for the moderns, she likes F. Scott Fitzgerald in the fiction field, and believes that Thornton Wilder is destined to take rank as one of the truly great modern playwrights. Andre Kostelanetz is her idea of what a modern musician should be, and her favorite song is *Night and Day*, which, incidentally, is the name of her favorite scent, a little something whipped up in the perfume line by Elizabeth Arden.

Jesse meets Marshal Wright to surrender.

Jesse meets Mr. McCoy, the railroad president, and learns that he is to be tried and executed.

Jesse behind bars.

Marshal Wright and deputy kill a member of the James gang.

Mr. McCoy pleads with Jesse to spare his life.

The militia rides after Jesse and Frank when they break out of jail.

Jesse discusses the possibility of robbing the Northfield, Minnesota bank with his gang.

Jesse and Frank meet in Northfield under assumed identities.

Jesse is wounded in the holdup.

Jesse and his gang flee from the bank.

Jesse makes his way back to St. Joseph.

Jesse and Zee embrace as they decide to go to California.

Jesse is shot by Robert Ford.

Jesse is dead.

Zee, Jesse James, Jr., and Marshal Wright attend the funeral of Jesse.

In Loving Remembrance

JESSE W. JAMES

Died April 3, 1882.

Aged 34 Years, 6 Months, 28 Days

Murdered By a Traitor and Coward
Whose Name is Not Worthy To
Appear Here.

Tombstone over Jesse's grave.

Both Nancy and her mother believe that whatever artistic talent has found its way into the Kellys comes from Nancy's mother's father, the late John C. Walsh, a renowned musician, who was, in his day, president of the National Musicians' Union.

Nancy never has so much as set foot in a dramatic school. She received all her training either at home, or in actual experience behind the footlights and before the camera and the microphone. But, as her mother says, "she was born with stage presence."

Five feet, five inches tall, she weighs 113 pounds, and her slim young figure requires no such attention as diet or exercise other than the kind she obtains in indulging in her favorite sports.

Her eyes are large and clear and the deep brown of forest pools; her hair is shiny, satiny brown; her complexion is like ivory; her hands are long, slender, shapely—artistic.

*****

BRIAN DONLEVY

Brian Donlevy looks more like a handsome prizefighter than an actor, but the young Irishman who boasts the broadest shoulders in Hollywood and a muscular, well-knit physique has had many years of acting experience to fit him for his present screen career, which he pursues under contract to 20th Century-Fox.

Twelve years of successful work in Broadway plays fitted him for a try at the screen medium, and since he hit the film capitol in the middle of 1935, he has had very few idle moments.

Donlevy was born in Portadown, County Armagh, Ireland, on February 9th. His father was a maker of Irish whiskey who gave up that business when Brian was 10 months old, to come to the United States and enter the woolen business. He died in 1933. His mother lives in Sheboygan Falls, Wisconsin.

Brian went to school in Sheboygan Falls, Beaver Dam, Cleveland, St. John's Military Academy in Dalefield, Wisconsin, and at the United States Naval Academy.

As a youngster in Cleveland he wrote poetry. His failure to conceal his interest in poetry led to considerable fighting and although he lost a good many decisions at first he later became sufficiently competent to fight professionally.

Incidentally, Donlevy, still writes poetry but admits his ability in this line never did improve.

Somebody gave Brian a bugle just after the family had established itself in Beaver Dam and he attributes to bugle blowing the barrel-like design of his chest.

When a Wisconsin national guard unit lost its bugler, Brian was permitted to substitute. When the company was sent to join Pershing on his Mexican Punitive Expedition young Donlevy talked himself into the trip—as a member. His height and weight made it possible for him to get away with his lie about his age. He ran away from home.

Nine months later the boys came home and Brian's parents decided to let their son confine his military fervor to a military school and he was sent to St. John's. He was not quite 14 when he came home from school and announced he was going to join the Lafayette Escandrille.

In France he learned to fly and became a sergeant-pilot. He spent three years doing patrol duty and pursuit flying. He was wounded twice, once in the head and once in the leg.

At the time he suffered the head wound he says he remembers only that things went black before his eyes and when he regained consciousness, perhaps a few seconds later, blood was streaming down his face. He landed his ship and then discovered he had set it down in front of a hospital.

After the war he returned home, finished four year's work in two and received an appointment to Annapolis. He left after a year when he learned that four years to sea duty would have to precede his transfer to a flying branch of the service. He did not flunk out.

While at Annapolis he engaged in Academy theatricals and when he decided he would have to sacrifice his plans to fly he went to New York to find out if he could make good on the stage.

But while Brian was interested in the stage, the theatre did not appear to be interested in him. While engaged in hounding theatrical agents he looked up Leyendecker, the illustrator, with whom he had maintained a correspondence of sorts the day he bumped his head on a Leyendecker poster in a French dugout.

Leyendecker gave him some work posing for a series of collar and cigarette ads to help keep the wolf on the right side of the door. The artist also recommended Donlevy join the Green Room Club where he might meet theatrical people. Brian joined and, among others, met the late Louis Wolheim who took a liking to him and put him in the cast of *What Price Glory* as the corporal.

From that moment his steps led upward and he went from one successful show to another, playing comedies, farces, dramas and musical comedies.

Those plays in which he appeared include *Rainbow, Queen Bee, Up Pops the Devil, Peter Flies High, Hit the Deck, Society Girl, The Inside Story, Three Cornered Moon, Three and One, No Questions Asked, The Perfumed Lady, The Milky Way* and others.

He came to Hollywood to play the role of the prize fighter in Harold Lloyd's screen version of *The Milky Way* but the picture was delayed, and, calling on his friend, Bob McIntyre, Samuel Goldwyn's casting director, he was induced into the cast of *Barbary Coast* as the black shirted killer.

He is nearly six feet tall but, because of his breadth and thickness, doesn't look it. He weighs 190 pounds, has light brown hair and gray-green eyes.

His middle name is Waldo, but it's dangerous to kid him about it.

He was married to Marjorie Lang, actress-singer, at Ensenada, Mexico, on December 22, 1936 and was remarried in a religious ceremony performed by Dr. Willsie Martin at the Wilshire Methodist Episcopal Church at high-noon December 31, 1936. Eleanor Powell, M. G. M. dancing star was the bride's only attendant, and producer Sol M. Wurtzel was the groom's best man.

*****

JOHN CARRADINE

A few years ago, Hollywood citizens used to point with civic pride to their two most unique characters—a duet of gentlemen who valiantly, if unconsciously, did more than most to color drab Hollywood Boulevard.

These men were Peter, the Hermit, a reincarnated Moses, even to the flowing white robes, sandals and staff—a resurrection of many dead centuries who marched unseeing and with imperious insolence down that street of a thousand aches. The other was John Carradine, as tall as Peter was short and as cadaverously thin and hungry as Cassius.

Peter, the Hermit, was silent on his daily trudges down the Boulevard, but not so Carradine. With a scraggly beard bending to the smallest breeze, he would recite choice passages from Shakespeare in a hypnotic voice that drowned the tramping of a thousand feet—a man walking in a trance of sublime indifference.

The Hermit has strangely disappeared from the Boulevard these past few months, but the curious have found him resting in the primitive hills to the north of town, hovering mother-like over his dogs. And Carradine, the Shakespeare of Hollywood, no longer shouts his lines in defiance of man-made noises; he's an actor now, and quite an important one.

In the space of a very few months, Bohemian Carradine has crossed several Rubicons. At a time when life was considerably bleaker than usual for even his optimistic soul, Darryl F. Zanuck of 20th Century-Fox gave him a contract and a chance to mutter portentous threats through his thin beard at Warner Baxter in *The Prisoner of Shark Island*.

Much experience hissing the mere insidious Shakespearian sybillants has made him an extremely competent menace—a menace is an actor who, in the old days, used to twirl his handlebar mustaches and foreclose mortgages. In this type of acting the Shakespeare of Hollywood has no competition whatsoever.

As a super villain he is well equipped with a lean and saturnine countenance and a thrilling and vibrant voice that drips with honey or menace, depending on which faucet he turns on. This voice of his can frighten children as it did Shirley Temple in *Captain January*. The Hollywood Shakespeare was assigned to hiss a warning in this film and did it so well Zanuck took it out.

Five years of buffeting against Hollywood Boulevard's cold indifference gives a man the ability to take it with a grin. John Carradine positively laughed with joy when Zanuck's decision reached his ears.

"Finally I have achieved success," he intoned. There was a Shakespearian phrase to fit that phase of his life, but in the excitement of being recognized for his sinister talent, Carradine forgot it. All that sufficed for him was that his voice had achieved distinction along with Boris Karloff's on a cloudy night. The fact that his virtue was slightly negatived by cutting room antics didn't bother him a bit.

As a matter of fact, that voice has played him some mean tricks. A few years ago Cecil B. DeMille, while passing down the Boulevard saw an apparition pass him. What interested him intensely was that the man was reciting the grave digger's lines from Hamlet with a finesse to be expected of a Sir Henry Irving and an Edwin Booth.

Mr. DeMille bustled to catch up and when he did he instructed Carradine to report to him the following day. The director was casting odd types for *The Sign of the Cross*, and Carradine seemed to sense this for he hesitated for a moment. After all, he had sacrificed many things for his art and being an extra wasn't his idea of success, neither was being an extra to be sneezed at, so he hemmed and hawed and accepted.

He appeared the following day in sack cloth and during the recording of mob noises, his deep baritone vibrated the sensitive ears of the maestro. Then DeMille dropped his microphone, for he had discovered a rare voice indeed. And so it came about that the Shakespeare of Hollywood, with a polish to his shoes and a tailored shave, recited the Beatitudes which later were transposed into the mouth of Herbert Brunson.

And so Carradine became a ghost voice. Those who remember that picture still thrill to the quasi-mad *Not Death, but Victory* that rang out from the multitude of Christian martyrs being led to the

122

lions. Our Mr. Carradine was that voice. A few years later he ghosted more lines in *The Crusades* and a few months ago, unseen by the camera, he spoke President McKinley's stirring lines which dispatched *The Message to Garcia*.

These five precarious years on Hollywood Boulevard prove one point, that this fellow was a courageous man. Jobs were scarcer than the milk of kindness and there were times when beds were remote as jobs. During the depressive weeks he used to solace himself marching up the Boulevard with Shakespeare. Report has it that he used to strike one-sided bargains with restaurant owners. The proposition being this: In return for four hour's work washing dishes he would be glad to accept a meal. Carradine is an actor now—on the very threshold of distinction—and in view of this we shouldn't pry too heavily into the past. At any rate, he survived.

Into this bare existence crept more than one heroic note. Remember that he was Hollywood's only exponent of the philosphy of many great artists who subscribed, through necessity, to the romantic notion that men of genius must starve. Reciting Shakespeare became a sort of mental food for the casting of physical pangs.

Some of the finest things done at Pasadena's celebrated Community Playhouse with Shakespeare were concerned with this same Carradine. Often so pressed for nickels that he couldn't purchase a trolley ride, he would thumb his way to the Playhouse for weeks on end and play *Hamlet* as a star.

Now it is the highest of distinctions to be invited as a star at this Playhouse. There is no carfare, only praise from a jeweled audience. No one who saw this series of Shakespearean plays suspected for a minute that Carradine was the Boulevard sage beloved of visiting firemen.

During this period of artistic affluence, he obtained a ticket to a Los Angeles production of *Hamlet*. Patiently he waited through the first act for the appearance of Hamlet. When he failed to show, Carradine rose with great dignity and denounced the producer as a fraud. The Mayor of the City of Los Angeles was there and he had made the mistake of applauding this travesty.

"And you, Mr. Mayor," reported Carradine, "should know better than to lend your presence to this fraud. You ought to be ashamed of yourself."

As a consequence of this, he was surrounded by policemen and escorted none too roughly to a sergeant's desk, where he stayed only a few minutes. The producer of *Hamlet* was put in jail for a month and Mayors of the City of Los Angeles no longer lend their persons to unsponsored productions of Shakespeare.

At this stage of the game, Carradine no longer quotes neat passages from the Bard of Avon. The need for this is past. John Carradine is finally on the threshold of his destiny; he's an actor now.

Carradine was born at Greenwich Village, New York City on February 5th, under the name Richmond Reed Carradine. His father, William Reed Carradine, was a newspaperman, stationed with the Associated Press in London. His mother, Genevieve Winifred Richmond Carradine, is a physician. His grandfather, Dr. Beverly Carradine, was co-founder of the Holiness Methodist Church, better known as the Holy Rollers.

Although he never has been to England, for many years he was mistaken for an Englishman—a belief he materially aided by inventing a biography dripping with missing "H's", and "Rawther's."

While he never studied art, his facility with a brush brought him to the theatre as a scene painter. He was by turn a quick-sketch artist and a designer. He is a sculptor after a fashion.

Five years of this sketching and designing went by and Carradine decided to become an actor. He applied for the Christ-like part of the stranger in *Window Panes* with Sara Padden and was given instead the comedy role of *Peter*, a simple-minded Russian peasant. The engagement was a success, so he headed for Hollywood by the hitch-hike route. He started out, flat broke and with just the clothes on his back.

"I made excellent time until I reached Shreveport, La., where I laid over for a spell. Every large town I would hit, I hunted up an art store and borrowed paper and a drawing board. Then I would canvass the office buildings, persuading the busy executives to pose for a quick sketch. I usually charged $2.50 each, and I would make as high as $15 a day. In this way I could live in the best of hotels, but depending upon my one faultless outfit to hitch rides.

"I worked in Shreveport, New Orleans, Dallas and El Paso as a quick-sketch artist, interspersed with jobs running art galleries.

"I never had studied art, but I learned enough about painting, etching and sculpture to pass as an expert."

"The last leg of my journey—El Paso to Los Angeles—I was riding in style in a chair car as a banana messenger. He's the courier who accompanies banana trains carrying the necessary way bills and such."

There was no welcoming committee to greet Carradine when he arrived in Hollywood, so he turned to the "little theatre" groups, appearing in a string of Shakespearean festivals, such as *Merry Wives of Windsor, Romeo and Juliet, King John, King Henry IV*, and finally starring in *Richard III*. He also played the role of Judas in the Pilgrimage Play in 1930.

Carradine is tall and spare, almost ascetic in appearance. He is six feet one inch tall, and weighs 150 pounds.

Late in 1935 he was married to Ardonelle Cosner and has one son by this marriage, John Arthur Carradine. Shortly after they were married, Carradine legally adopted Mrs. Carradine's son by a previous marriage. The four-year-old lad is now called Bruce Carradine.

With no prospects for a job in Hollywood, he began that era of eccentricity which made him one of the most unique figures ever to pass along Hollywood Boulevard.

*****

JANE DARWELL

All the sobs and struggles in Jane Darwell's life are those she experienced vicariously during her stage and screen career. Probably the only actress in filmdom whose life and career, she thankfully admits, have been without hardship, the amazing diversity and perfection of her portrayals are due entirely to intelligent observation, emotional comprehension and an apparently unlimited ability to visualize and recreate her concept of each character she enacts.

Miss Darwell became an overnight screen favorite two years ago through her unforgettable performance as the tough but warm-hearted head nurse in *The White Parade*. Since then her career has been a succession of small but brilliant and finely etched screen portraits.

It is a paradox of Movieland that Miss Darwell, member of an aristocratic family, should spend her film days playing the roles of nurses, cooks, housekeepers. Yet she not only enjoys the roles but puts all her love and talent into the characterizations.

Miss Darwell was born Patti Woodward at Palmyra, Missouri, where her family maintained a summer home. Her birthday is October 15—also, she humorously tells, the birthday of Sara Bernhardt and John L. Sullivan. Her father was W. R. Woodward, one of the Louisville and Southern and of the Toronto, Hamilton and Buffalo railroads. Her mother was Ellen Booth, whose father was Presbyterian minister at Seymour, Indiana.

Her family moved from Louisville to Chicago when she was four-years-old, and her education began there at the Douglas Public School. At various times she attended Miss Loring's private school in Chicago, Miss Annie Noll's School at Louisville, Kentucky, and graduated from exclusive Dana Hall in Boston, where she took up the study of voice and piano and continued her music lessons for close to six years in Boston and Chicago with a view to operatic roles, although she admits her earliest ambition was to become a circus performer.

Miss Darwell had her first taste of theatricals at Dana Hall, where

126

she invariably took boys' roles in school days, principally because her sister-in-law's brother's clothes fitted her so perfectly! Even then she specialized in comedy characterizations, and because of her flair for farce as well as the high quality of her mezzo soprano voice, she was offered a contract with The Bostonians, a light opera company. Her father refused to grant his permission for anything so undignified as a stage career, and the young Jane—or "Patsy," as she was called before she adopted her professional name—was so angry that she didn't sing again for three years, although she never failed to attend every operatic symphonic and other musical event which came to Boston. Sent abroad on a pleasure trip to forget her disappointment, Miss Darwell took advantage of courses in dramatics and voice in various European cities.

The family frequently wintered in California, but it was not until she was visiting a brother in Chicago that she decided, suddenly, to become an actress. Her decision took root while she was witnessing a performance of *Sherlock Holmes* at the Chicago Opera House by the Chicago Stock Company, in which Bessie Barriscale and Howard Hickman were featured. At the conclusion of the performance she went back stage and talked Clark Bellows, manager of the show, into giving her a part in his next production, *The Stubbornness of Geraldine*. Miss Darwell still believes she got the role simply because it required an extravagant wardrobe, which the company couldn't afford, and which she herself possessed. At any rate she won the part, did a good job of it, and played second leads during the remainder of the season in such plays as *The Girl With the Green Eyes, The Dancing Girl* and *The Cowboy and the Lady*.

Following this she traveled abroad for three years, visiting friends in England, Germany, Russia, France, Belgium, Austria and Holland. In her numerous journeys abroad in subsequent years, she re-visited these countries, Bermuda and Honolulu, as well as motoring all over the United States, but she has never visited Italy, and hopes some day to journey there.

Returning to this country, she led the life of a typical debutante enjoying the social whirl in Chicago and nearby resorts, cruising along the New England coast or Florida, attending polo matches at Honolulu, the Belmont horse races in New York, or riding the thoroughbred pacers in her father's stables on his huge Iron Mountain

Ranch, a hundred miles from St. Louis.

Visiting her brother again in Los Angeles, with no intention of embarking on a motion picture career, she happened to meet Oscar Apfel, who was director of the Chicago Stock Company when she was one of its players. Apfel, at the moment, was directing silent pictures for Jesse L. Lasky and he induced her to sign a contract. Her very first screen role, however, was that of an old Philippine servant in Henry McRae's *The Capture of Aguinaldo*, in which she rode a western pony at breakneck speed. With Mr. Lasky's company, she was featured for two years in such films as *The Master Mind, Brewster's Millions* and *The Only Son*.

At that time the stage was considered superior to the screen and since she found a professional career infinitely more interesting than a social one, at the expiration of her contract Miss Darwell accepted an offer to go to San Francisco with Bert Lytoll's company, appearing at the Alcazar Theatre there for several years in *The Only Son* and a succession of stock successes.

Later, she joined John Halliday for a season at Sacramento; and was with the Thomas Wilkes organization in Seattle, before she headed for New York, where she opened at the National Theatre with Jose Ruben and Claire Eames in Sidney Howard's play, *Swords*. Then she did *Turn to the Right* and *East Is West* for Henry Duffy, made several excursions into stock with B. F. Keith throughout New Hampshire, with Albee's stock company at Providence, Rhode Island, and for three years in Detroit with the Woodward Players.

On June 7, 1930, she arrived back in Hollywood, and was promptly tested and signed by Paramount for the role of the Widow Douglas in *Tom Sawyer* and *Huckleberry Finn*. Since then she has made a formidable series of pictures but it was not until her splendid depiction of the nurse, Sailor in *The White Parade* that she was acclaimed as a great character actress and signed to a contract by the then Fox Film Company.

During her career, she has played every type of role, but she prefers such character roles as she played in *White Fang, Ramona, McFadden's Flats, Star for a Night* and *Laughing at Trouble* to any she has done on stage or screen. She particularly loves dialect roles, and has an amazing number of dialects at her command.

Filled with energy, Miss Darwell prefers to be working at all times. She is a polo, football, horse race and fight fan; fond of motoring, and confesses she was nursing the idea of becoming a nun at the time the stage bug hit her.

She is a direct descendant on her father's side, of Andrew Jackson, and among her possessions is a set of gaffs the former president used during his cock fighting activities.

She loves to read; biographies interest her most. Likes a good comedy character role—with a tear in it.

She lives in Hollywood with her brother, W. C. Woodward, a retired business man, and Mary Stoneham, a 14-year-old niece. She raises St. Bernard dogs, but likes a variety of animals around. At present, her personal menagerie consists of Patsy, a St. Bernard; Pooch, an Australian sheep dog; Bridget, a great dane; Nancy, a cocker spaniel she purchased from Don Hill, prop man on *Star for a Night* set; a "raft of cats" including Mary Jane Twinkletoes, Jane Withers, Disraeli, Dearest, Rags, a tortoise shell cat, Rags and Second, Dagwood, Blondie and Sistie, who is the mother of all the other felines. She eats vegetables, fruit and nuts grown on her own acre, specializes in raising silver lace Wyandotte chickens, of which she has 50; there are 10 game banties, two tame baby humming birds, a number of turkeys, ducks and Rhode Island reds who stroll blissfully through the Darwell gardens, too. Miss Darwell hopes to mate Patsy, the St. Bernard, to Buck, famed canine film actor.

She loves fresh flower perfumes, and loathes heavy or exotic scents; blue in any shade is her favorite color; she is obsessed by no superstitions; she is always perfectly groomed; attends every concert at the Hollywood Bowl, and every vocal music event in Los Angeles; the one thing she would have liked to be is an opera singer; although she no longer sings or plays herself, she is a rabid collector of opera singers' autographs, and will go anywhere any time to get a glimpse of Grace Moore, Lily Pons, Gladys Swarthout and Rosa Ponselle.

Although she's played probably more cook roles than anyone on the screen today, she doesn't like cooking and knows nothing about it except one recipe—her favorite dish—Lamb Chile, which she learned from her brother's wife, the former Margaret Winston, a Spanish lady who is a cousin of Leo Carrillo and a grandchild of the famous Bandini.

She is so fond of horses—her family used to own a famous stable

129

of trotters and pacers—that she would like to do a story of a woman who runs a home for jockeys at a racetrack.

She is proud of the artistic talent of her niece, Mary Stoneham, who draws animals so expertly, Miss Darwell hopes she may become a second Rosa Bonheur.

Although she weighs 165 pounds, Miss Darwell has never bothered about dieting, claiming she never made good until she became stout.

She is unmarried—but has a mother complex. Always has from one to four of her nieces and their friends living with her. Adores shopping for them and supervising their education, and thinks its good for them to live in her "funny old ranch house" with live things growing around them, instead of attending exclusive private schools.

Miss Darwell is five feet, five and a half inches tall, has exceedingly blue eyes, and dark brown hair streaked with gray.

*****

J. EDWARD BROMBERG

Unless one watches out for him, it is hard to recognize J Edward Bromberg from one picture to another. This young character actor, in his early thirties, has played everything from gray-haired old scientists to dashing young go-getter enthusiasts—and rarely does he act his age.

Acting and the stage were like his own life's blood to him, and when Bromberg was signed up by 20th Century-Fox, he approached Hollywood and the movies with the trepidation of one embarking on an unknown adventure.

For all but two years of his life, Bromberg had been a resident of New York City where he learned to become a disillusioned realist. The fantasy of Hollywood opened a new sort of life for him to learn.

He was born on Christmas Day, December 25, in the city of Temesvar, Hungary, the son of Herman Bromberg and Josephine Roth. Just two years after his birth the family moved to America, settling immediately in New York City where his father was a prominent welfare worker. The only interruption came, when at the age of six, he was taken back for a short visit to his native Hungary, at which time he got the only remembered impression of this land and the greatest thrill which he has ever experienced. To show how serene his life has been since then, this thrill consisted of lifting the blinds of his window on the train and getting his first glimpse of the city of his birth in the form of a cluster of lights at night.

With this constituting his greatest thrill, he also confesses that he cannot remember suffering any great disappointments.

His school days were uneventful, for he devoted all his time and interest to his studies, eventually excelling in English and the Arts. After graduation from Public School No. 10 in the Bronx and Stuyvesant High School, he spent two years at City College of New York before getting out into the world to earn his living.

Throughout his school years, there was a vague desire at the back of his head to become an actor, but he then had no idea as to how he could accomplish it. Instead, he spent the first eight years of his wage-

131

earning life as the silk salesman, candy manufacturer and laundry worker. With each succeeding job his distaste for this kind of work deepened, and his desire to become an actor crystalized into a firm resolve. For two years, he studied acting with the stage director, Bulgakov, and was finally rewarded with a small part in the Provincetown Theatre production of *Princess Turandot*.

This broke the ice for him—but not sufficiently. Soon after that he tried to become definitely professional by applying to Eva Le Gallienne's Civic Repertory group on 14th Street for a job. There was nothing open for him there, but he was advised to join the student group, get some training and await developments. He did not have long to wait. There was a part to be filled in a play and he was recommended to Miss Le Gallienne as one of the best prospects for it.

That started five unbroken years of work with the Civic Repertory Theatre, during which time he appeared in such plays as *Romeo and Juliet* in which he played Mercutio, Chekhov's *Three Sisters* and *The Cherry Orchard, Bourgeois Gentleman, Twelfth Night, Peter Pan*, in which he played Nana, the dog, and *Lady from Alfa Queque*.

In 1930 he broke this long association to accept an engagement from Jed Harris to play in *The Inspector General* with Dorothy Gish. This was one of his only two "short term" engagements, for right after that, in 1931, he joined the Group Theatre, from which he was recently recruited for the movies by 20th Century-Fox.

There he made his first appearance in *The House of Connelly* with Franchot Tone. After that he played in *1931, Night Over Taos* and *Big Night*. Following the latter play in 1933, he made his other interlude, appearing with Walter C. Kelly in the Theater Guild production of *Both Your Houses*.

His next performance with the Group Theatre, in the role of Dr. Hochberg in *Men in White* won him the award of one of the best stage performances of the year 1934. His next plays were *Gold Eagle Guy, Awake and Sing, Waiting for Lefty* and finally, *Weep for the Virgins* one of the rare "flops" in his career, which folded up after a week on the boards.

During the early part of his stage career on Sept. 3, 1927, he married Goldie Doberman, a non-professional, by whom he now has two children, Marcia, 7½ years old, and Conrad, 5½ years old.

Outside of his stage work, and now his screen work, he has no exciting activities. His great passion is chess, which he plays whenever and wherever possible, and reads every book which he can find on the subject. His favorite exercise is fencing, with swimming running a close second. Next to books on chess, his favorite reading matter is sociology, politics and economics.

He brings with him to Hollywood one of the oddest of hobbies. For years he has been collecting unusual shoes, slippers and sandals, and he welcomed the trip West because it opened new territory in which he could search for additions to his collection. Besides this, he collects phonograph recordings of the world's best records. This collection has more practical use, for he is a great lover of music, his favorite composition being Beethoven's fourth piano concerto, and his favorite orchestra the New York Philharmonic.

His favorite play is *The Cherry Orchard* by Anton Chekhov in which he once played, but his favorite role is that of Dr. Hochberg in *Men in White*. He rates as the best motion picture he has seen the Russian film, Chapayev.

He goes into ecstasies over a dish of frog legs sec, and rates red as his favorite color.

He is a rare exception among stage and screen folk for he has not a single superstition.

In painting, he rates Giotto as his favorite classical painter, and Cezanne among the moderns.

Shakespeare takes his first choice in playwriting, with Cifford Odets, author of *Awake and Sing* and *Waiting for Lefty* in which Bromberg appeared, as his favorite modern playwright.

Among the authors, old and new, he names Dostoyefsky and Romaine Rolland as his favorites, with Toulouse-Lautrec as his choice of illustrators. Watt Tyler is his idea of a great historical character.

There is no type of person he admires more than one who creates, no matter in what field it is, while his greatest aversion is pretension.

His idea of the ideal vacation is a world cruise, which he hopes to take some day.

Not only is he free from superstition, but he does not believe in hunches and has never followed one.

He always manages to sleep an average of eight hours nightly, and attends the movies once a week for relaxation.

Being new to screen work, he has yet to define his desires in this direction. Thus far, all of his thoughts are with the stage. His greatest ambition is to be able to reach the point where he can act in the theatre without it being also an economic necessity. He wants to be independent enough financially so that he can do the things he wants to on the stage.

There is only one great fear which haunts him, and that is the thought of ever being physically incapable of working.

He is 5 feet 7½ inches in height, weighs 180 pounds, has brown hair and brown eyes.

*****

CHARLES TANNEN

Charles Tannen, son of humorist Julius Tannen, wanted to be a studio publicity writer and was forced to become a screen actor instead.

Young Tannen arrived in Hollywood fully prepared "to knock the town on its ear with a swell publicity stunt *Munity on the Bounty*, but Ida Koverman, to whom he divulged his gigantic exploitation scheme, looked instead of listened and asked him if he would take a film test.

Disgusted, but broke, he admitted he might even go so far as to turn actor, took his test and a month later started "on the road to a writer's ruin" in the role of the blind boy in *The Dark Angel*, with Frederic March and Merle Oberon.

Tannen who was born in New York City, October 22, educated at Lawrenceville Preparatory School where he was editor on *The Lawrence*, the newspaper founded by Owen Johnson, started his professional writing career on the staff of the New York *Herald-Tribune*, covering county court cases during his summer vacation. When his famous father went to Chicago to pinch-hit for Ben Bernie at the College Inn, Charles accompanied him, becoming Bernie's press agent when the latter arrived.

After a year with Bernie, he returned to New York, secured a job with the Lehman Brothers' banking house, where he did publicity for polo player Tommy Hitchcock until the latter fell off a horse and broke his back. About to lose his job, he pleaded for a chance in the financial department, where he worked for a year and of which he admits he still knows nothing.

It was then that he came to Hollywood, won his first role as an actor and continues to assuage his literary pride by turning out short stories and scenarios between pictures.

A good bit in *Fighting Youth* at Universal was followed by another in *Ship Cafe*, in which he did so well that two scenes were added to the original brief appearance he was to have made in the film with Mady Christians and Carl Brisson. Small parts in *Ah, Wilderness* and *Small Town Girl* brought him to the attention of Darryl Zanuck, who signed him to a 20th Century-Fox contract.

An attractive youth, he confesses he now enjoys acting and hopes some day to be as good as his idol, Burgess Meredith, star of the New York stage production *Winterset*. Fond of swimming, golf, monopoly and tennis—he was a member of the Lawrenceville Prep School Tennis Team—a number of his short stories have been published nationally, his favorite being *The Friday Morning After*, which appeared in Esquire nearly two years ago.

Five feet, ten and a half inches tall, Charles is blue-eyed, blonde-haired, weighs 157 pounds, and would like, ultimately, to be in either the writing or production end of the motion picture business.

*****

JOHNNIE RUSSELL

At the age of 5, when nearly all other children are busy in the kindergarten, manly little Johnnie Russell is busy carving out a career in Hollywood. And if eager interest and precocious ability count for anything, Master Johnnie seems destined to go far.

A typical American boy is this blonde, blue-eyed youngster whom chance, working through a real estate broker who remains anonymous, set on the road to juvenile stardom.

He is appealing; he is active and he is mischievous. He likes spinach but can't quite get enthusiastic over carrots and he's seldom too tired to romp or play with other children, if they are about, or with adults in case playmates of his own age are lacking.

Aside from the fact that his hair is cut rather long, there is nothing superficially to distinguish him from the average small boy. But when he takes his place before the camera, the difference becomes obvious even to the unpracticed eye. For he then demonstrates an ability to follow direction, fall into mood and go through gesture and dialogue much beyond his five years.

The tale of Johnnie's rise in the film firmament forms one of those minor success epics only possible in Hollywood.

Johnnie is the son of Mr. and Mrs. H. R. Countryman of New York. He is an only child. His father is art editor of the Associated Press in New York in which capacity he is in charge of all pictures that are obtained and sent out to clients by this greatest of all world news gathering agencies.

Until his advent in Hollywood, the boy was a child model for some two years in New York. He demonstrated children's clothes and posed for artists and thereby received considerable preliminary training for the screen.

But in November, 1937, Mrs. Countryman decided to visit California for a vacation. She naturally took her small son along.

Here chance and real estate broker entered the picture. Mrs. Countryman, intending to spend some time in Hollywood, set about looking for a home. She called in a real estate man to help her. Chance led them to a house just vacated and but a few doors removed from the home of Mrs. Wright Felt, mother of little Joan Carol, the winsome little child actress under contract to 20th Century-Fox. Mrs. Countryman liked the house and leased it. As might be expected, little Joan and Johnnie met at play and became fast friends. That led to a friendship between the two mothers and Johnnie's first break in the movies.

At Mrs. Felt's suggestion, Mrs. Countryman had the boy take a test for a part in *The Duke Comes Back* a prize fight story and the boy promptly was awarded the role. Then came an interval of waiting and Mrs. Countryman was preparing to return to her home in New York when she was advised by Mrs. Felt that 20th Century-Fox was eagerly questing for a boy of Johnnie's approximate age for one of the year's most important child roles in *Always Goodbye*.

A special production with an all-star cast which included such names as Barbara Stanwyck, Herbert Marshall, Cesar Romero, Ian Hunter and Lynn Bari, the picture was being held in abeyance for want of a child about whom the entire story revolved.

Some 400 boys between the ages of 4½ and 7 had been tested by the studio over a month's period before little Johnnie popped into the scene. There were 89 children left to test, among them the small son of Arline Judge, noted film actress, and the little brother of Pauline Moore, another film celebrity.

But when the final tests were completed, Johnnie walked off with the part. Darryl F. Zanuck, studio production chief, Lew Schreiber, casting head, and Sidney Lanfield, the director of *Always Goodbye*, unanimously settled on him after seeing the tests.

*****

TYRONE POWER'S LOCATION DIARY

Thrills and humor in this intimate record of the filming of Jesse James—by the star himself! As it appeared in **Screenland** *magazine.*

August 26th.

What a day. And what a trip! Not my first location trip, but one that promises to be as exciting as the picture I'm going to make. Director Henry King is, like myself, air-minded. We left Hollywood this morning in his streamlined Waco cabin cruiser, one of the swankiest I've ever seen, and here we are, right over the greenswept Ozarks, almost at our destination. All through the trip I couldn't help thinking how lucky I've been with one grand part after the other during the past year. And now, to top it all, *Jesse James*, crammed full of action and romance. My fellow players are just about tops. Henry Fonda is my screen brother, Frank James; Nancy Kelly, a grand girl and a real actress, my screen wife; Randy Scott, the United States Marshal; Jane Darwell, my mother; Brian Donlevy, the landbuyer for the railroad, and all the rest. This location trip promises to be a swell one.

August 27th.

Reached the airport at Neosho, Missouri, yesterday and we roped the plane down to a barbed wire fence. Motored to Pineville, Missouri, where we're going to "shoot" most of the technicolor sequences and spent the night there. Nice country with beautiful unexpected vistas. Met some of Pineville's important people today, grand guys, all of them: Mayor Drumm, Lee Carnell, Sheriff Bone, C. A. Poindexter, editor of the Pineville *Democrat*, and other townsmen and farmers who came by car and wagon to see what changes Hollywood has made to this town. Pineville has a population of 383.

August 28th.

Today we looked for living quarters. We have 175 persons in our film company and although we will work in Pineville, the town hasn't enough accommodations for all of us. I found a room in a private home on the outskirts of Noel, Missouri, a picturesque summer resort town in the heart of the Ozarks, eleven miles away from Pineville by pavement, eight miles of gravel. Others of the troupe found nice accommodations here, too. Director King has a nice room in a beautiful white house, commanding a grand view of the little town and the majestic hills. (They're called mountains down here, but I mustn't take the word too seriously. In California we have mountains that are *real-*

141

ly colossal).

The rest of the troupe got in by train today, Hank Fonda, Donlevy, Nancy Kelly, Randy Scott, and the rest. The entire Ozark country gathered at the little brick station in Noel to welcome them. Sidney Bowen, our company business manager, had come ahead of us and had been busy throughout this region for weeks, hunting out places for the troupe to find room and board. They are all comfortably located, now, though scattered over the countryside. Our hosts are extremely hospitable. My own landlord tells me they've been having pretty hard times down this way—the arrival of our company was an economic Godsend—but there is no talk of defeat, no crying of the blues and no whining.

August 29th.

Actual filming started today. Our first scenes were made on the "old Crowder farm." It's a small place, run by the widow Crowder, who is one of the kindliest people I've ever met. The place offers so much scenically that George Barnes, our ace cameraman who is a veteran of many scenic locations in his time, broke down and turned on the exclamations. Naturally, Duke Green, our technicolor cameraman, was all het up about the color possibilities and had his camera set up in record time. It got pretty hot during the day, so Mrs. Crowder dipped up a big wooden bucket of clear, cold spring water for us. I've never had wine that tasted better, and the rest of us who worked today, Randy Scott, Hank Fonda, Brian Donlevy and Nancy Kelly agreed with me. The work seemed to me to go pretty well, and when the end of the day came Henry King had a big smile on his face. That means he's satisfied! I hope we can keep it up. King is a great guy and it's because of folks like him and Darryl Zanuck that I have learned to get over the haunting taste of beans, coffee and pie—which I got on the cuff in a New York beanery, while waiting for a chance to get on the stage, which opened the path to Hollywood. No, I can't ever forget that, and I'll be eternally grateful to those who gave me the opportunity to work for something more than beans and coffee.

August 30th—September 2nd.

Mrs. Crowder's two grown-up sons went to work for us today as bit players. For a sequence in the film, we had to toss a bomb into a big, rambling farm house and set it afire. (Not actually, just smoke to simulate flames). It became the duty of the Crowder boys to help us form an old-fashioned bucket brigade to put out the fire in their own home. They told me how our business manager had leased the farm, put a new roof on the house since a new roof treated with Hollywood's special paint looked more ancient than their old roof, and how all the neighboring farmers had stood around while Hollywood workmen built a duplicate of a bedroom in the farmhouse back of the barn. It was here they had to film the death scene of my film mother, Jane Darwell.

Sheriff Bone and his hard-working deputies roped off the front yard and the barnyard of the farm so the crowds would know where to stand while we were filming. The crowds, by the way, instead of making noises and spoiling scenes, were as helpful and co-operative as humanly possible. I've never known folks so mobile and easy to manage. I haven't been on many locations (except for *Suez* and *Lloyds of London*), but I venture to say no veteran of the screen—or, for that matter, the stage, ever saw such well-mannered crowds. There were days when as many as 50,000 people watched us making a scene.

September 3rd.

This is a special day on my calendar because I attended my first dance in Noel. It was at Shadow Lake where Mr. Marx Chaney runs a restful and picturesque resort. There is a big dance floor and dining room, overlooking crystal-clear Elk River. "Hank," Randy, Nancy, and the rest of us danced, not only among ourselves but with the girls of Noel. I've never been in a given area so crowded with good looking girls before in my life. It's true we have beautiful girls in Hollywood, but they are brought there from every place in the world. In the Ozarks, they just come by it naturally. Beauty, here, is pretty unanimous. There are plenty of autograph seekers, but it's fun writing in their books, on scraps of paper, hats, pocketbooks or anything they happen to have handy, because they are so appreciative. But the crowds—and the town is always crowded, for a mile or two around Noel one has difficulty in finding parking room—never bother us during mealtime. They wait until we are through and then become one of us for the evening, doing their best to make our stay a pleasant and happy one.

September 4th.

These next days are to be eventful ones. We're going to film the great train robbery and stage the big jail break from the little, old red-brick courthouse in Liberty, Missouri. We won't be in Liberty, actually, but in Pineville, which looks today more like yesterday's Liberty than the modern town of Liberty does. It took considerable work to make the town look that way. We built a big hotel, saloon, marshal's office, newspaper building, took down all the telephone poles and lines and put the lines underground. Old-fashioned board sidewalks were built over concrete ones and, what will never cease to amaze the visitor to Pineville, to say nothing of its citizens, the town's pavement was buried beneath six inches of dirt. Only last December, after generations of living with dusty, dirty streets, Pineville proudly unveiled its paved streets. And just a few months later, Hollywood's miracle finger found it out (after Director King had flown over 15,000 miles in search for just such a colorful, unspoiled countryside as this) and put thousands of truckloads of dirt over the pavement. Of course everything will be restored. The only thing we will leave behind will be the money spent with the good folks of this region and the thousands that the tourists are bringing in while we are here.

September 5th.

Henry King has an uncanny ability to discover and uncover things. Imagine finding a ten-mile stretch of railroad on the old Frisco line near Southwest City—eight miles from Noel! It was here he decided to film the great train robbery. King also discovered an old engine and three passenger cars that had been used in the time of the James Boys. They were all reworked, repainted and put in top condition for the filming. All this shop work was done in Little Rock.

I never will forget the thrill standing atop the coal tender with two big single-action 45's in my hand while the old-fashioned train shook, swayed and rumbled down the track—all the while the technicolor camera was recording the scene. I kept thinking of that other time, years back, when Jesse James really held up a train, only a few miles from the exact spot where we were re-enacting that scene in color. The roaring fire in the fire-box threw out a red-hot glare at every shovel of coal. I don't know whether it was the actual heat or the memory of that other historical episode in the nation's development that made my heart pound harder and the heat seem intense, but while I stood there, today, swaying with each lurch of the engine, I was thrilled to my boots. I've always loved trains but this was the first time I ever had a chance to ride on top of one and look down into the cab where all the interesting gadgets are located, where the throttle sends the train plunging ahead, where the bell and whistle ropes are located. It awakened memories of my childhood when I wanted to be an engineer more than anything in the world. The smoke and cinders didn't bother me at all. I enjoyed every ounce of wind that slashed against my bandanna-covered face. Somehow, I didn't feel as if I were making a motion picture today. Instead, I was having the time of my life.

September 6th.

Today we finished filming the train robbery. We had to rope off part of the track to keep the crowds back. There must have been more than 50,000 people packed against the ropes, just out of camera range. They came from almost every state in the Union, judging by their car licenses. Residents of the town of Southwest City rented their yards as parking lots and sold ice cold soda pop off their porches. When we moved on down the railroad several miles near a steep bluff, people, in high spirit of adventure and sport, tramped through the woods for four miles and came down a mountain side to watch the final holdup scenes. One enterprising farmer opened up a road through the woods by chopping out the undergrowth and then he charged 25 cents to drive down to the edge of the cliff.

A very pretty girl among the extra players (we used all local people for atmosphere roles and brought two baggage carloads of costumes of the Jesse James period for this purpose), asked me if she could get on the train instead of being in that crowd that greeted the arrival of the first train to Liberty, Mo. (We were using Southwest City as Liberty for this purpose).

"You see," she said simply, "I've never been on a train in my life before and this is the first chance I have ever had."

Her charm was so compelling that I took her to Director King at once. "Why, bless your soul," he exclaimed, "I should say you *can* get on that train." Director King not only put her on the train, but placed her right in the background of a shot involving Randy Scott and Donald Meek. She had on a beautiful blue dress and blue bonnet. You might look for her in the picture She was as happy as any person I have ever seen. I believe her "train ride" was as thrilling to her as my ride atop the swaying coal tender yesterday.

September 7th.

Used 500 people today for the big jail break sequence. So Pine-

145

ville was certainly bustling. Many old-timers told me nothing had stirred up the countryside so much since the Civil War and I believe them.

We only brought four Hollywood trained horses with us. The others we hired from various farmers throughout the region. We had to have an entire cavalry as the scene called for the town to be placed under martial law, and we had to break in the horses to stand at the hitching racks while guns were being fired. It didn't take them long to get used to the noise. Dadblamed (you see I'm slipping into the true local color of the region) if I don't think those horses want to cooperate, like their masters have been doing right along. We shot pistols and muskets several times and then played the scene without any trouble. We had to take every precaution because a horse can snap a bridle quickly and charge through a crowd, spreading havoc. We almost had that happen once on the Crowder farm when an automobile frightened one of the mounts who pulled down an old railing fence post and dashed madly about, with the railing thumping at the end of the tough reins. Jimmy Williams, a very clever horseman with our troupe, calmed the animal and removed the railing before anyone was hurt.

September 8th.

Day off today. Drove to Tulsa, Oklahoma, to see the sights. Tulsa is a fine modern, bustling city, located about 120 miles away from here. It was a swell ride, over good roads. Imagine my shock when I arrived there to discover that I had forgotten my money and had to make a telephone call back to Noel. I had a nickel to get the operator with in a pay booth, but when I wanted to put through a collect call the operator asked, "Who's calling?"

"Tyrone Power," I said.

"Quit your fooling," she said, "I'm a busy person. Give me your name and I'll put the call through."

I tried to explain, but the more I talked, the more complicated it became. By that time, the other operators were enjoying the conversation until one said, "It *is* Tyrone Power. I recognize his voice. I'd know it anywhere." Then I heard them laugh.

She insisted and put the call through for me. I learned her name, that she lived at Sands Springs, Oklahoma, and when I got back to Noel I invited her up to dinner as my guest. She came up and we had a grand evening, dining and dancing at the Shadow Lake resort. She

146

had dances with some of the other boys, too. I wrote her a letter on my stationery thanking her for such a charming and thoroughly delightful evening. I also gave her a autographed picture, in fair exchange, for I demanded one of hers. And one arrived by the next mail.

September 9th—15th.

You just can't hold up a movie company, even with rain! While we had had some fine weather to make our technicolor shots, the sky suddenly clouded up the other day and we had a heavy shower. The shower didn't last long but during the rain we continued filming. Robert Webb, first assistant director King, had made plans accordingly. You may remember that Webb, who has been Henry King's assistant on almost all of his recent pictures, won the Award from the Academy of Motion Picture Arts and Sciences this year for his work as an assistant director on *In Old Chicago.*

We filmed in a "cover set," an interior scene that can be filmed regardless of the outside weather. The particular scene was my first love scene with Nancy Kelly. I had just robbed the train, doubled back after eluding the posse and called on Nancy at her uncle's newspaper office. Her uncle is Col. Cobb (Henry Hull). I was caught in the office by United States Marshal Randolph Scott, who pretends not to recognize me, but gives me a none too veiled warning to leave that neck of the woods or be prepared to shoot it out at the next meeting. We had a swell time playing that scene. When the rain got too loud on the roof, we covered it with soft, absorbing canvas to deaden the noise and went right on acting.

While we filmed this and other interior scenes, the crowds continued to visit the sets. We had a lot of fun talking to the various people about the country, their problems, what they thought of pictures. I'm sure we all profited as much for our talks with them as they did watching us play our scenes for *Jesse James.* During occasional showers, we would let the people stand on the porches and under what cover we had. Others brought their own umbrellas and stood patiently in the rain to watch us. It's kind of touching, such devotion, and is bound to make us feel a little humble.

September 15th.

Hank Fonda and I went fishing today. We both threw out lines over the rowboat gunwhale into the sparkling clear waters of the Elk River, bedded with gravel and huge slabs of clean, limestone rocks,

while the banks are beautiful white cliffs. I rowed awhile and kept a
weather eye on the line, but my vigil was unrewarded. Hank had more
luck, however, for suddenly his cork was jerked under with a splash.
Hank grabbed the line and started to tug. I was busy rowing the boat
and just at that time the boat *would* have to spring a leak. I started
bailing frantically while Fonda fought with the fish. We both won—I
kept the boat from sinking in midstream while Hank landed a beautiful seven-pound channel catfish. We didn't get to do any more fishing because the telephone at nearby Shadow Lake resort rang and we
were called back to the set for another scene.

September 16th.

We're on our way back to Hollywood with most of the scenes we
wanted safely in the can. Throughout our stay we worked every day
except for the one I got off to go to Tulsa. We were up every morning
at 4:30 or 5:00, had breakfast, made up, donned our costumes and
were on the set at Pineville or the Crowder Farm eleven miles away by
8 A.M. We worked straight through until six or seven every night, depending upon the sun. It was grand fun, every minute of it, for all of
us. In the end we left because the crowds, though very sensible and
reasonable, just got too big. Traffic was tied up, business was at a
standstill, and standing crops were getting trampled, so we had to pull
up stakes and get back to Hollywood. We leave, I think, with nothing
but happy memories, of the place, the people and of the work we managed to get done there. My only hope is that the people we lived with
and among during the filming of *Jesse James* will always remember
how much their rich and charming hospitality has meant to the entire
troupe. Now we're all on tenterhooks, waiting to see how that beautiful scenery shows up in technicolor. Bet it'll be swell!